The role of retrieval inhibition in directed forgetting -

an event-related brain potential analysis

ISBN: 3-9807282-2-6

Druck: Sächsisches Digitaldruck Zentrum, Dresden

Titelbild: "An unforgettable event - Stromboli, September 1998", © Markus Ullsperger, 1998

The role of retrieval inhibition in directed forgetting - an event-related brain potential analysis

(Die Rolle der Hemmung des Gedächtnisabrufs beim intentionalen Vergessen - eine Analyse ereigniskorrelierter Hirnpotentiale)

DISSERTATION

zur Erlangung des akademischen Grades

Dr. med.

an der Medizinischen Fakultät

der Universität Leipzig

eingereicht von:

Markus Ullsperger

geboren am 22. April 1970 in Berlin

angefertigt am:

Max-Planck-Institut für neuropsychologische Forschung

Betreuer:

Prof. Dr. med. D. Yves von Cramon

Beschluß über die Verleihung des Doktorgrades vom: 17.10.2000

Bibliographische Beschreibung:

Ullsperger, Markus

The role of retrieval inhibition in directed forgetting - an event-related brain potential analysis

(Die Rolle der Hemmung des Gedächtnisabrufs beim intentionalen Vergessen - eine Analyse ereigniskorrelierter Hirnpotentiale)

Universität Leipzig, Dissertation

126 S., 155 Lit., 16 Abb., 11 Tab., 1 Anlage

Referat:

Die verminderte Wiedererkennensleistung von zu vergessenden Wörtern in Gedächtnisaufgaben mit intentionalem Vergessen wird entweder auf differentielle Enkodierung oder auf Inhibitionsmechanismen auf der Ebene des Gedächtnisabrufes zurückgeführt. Ziel der vorliegenden Untersuchung war es, beide Erklärungsansätze mit Hilfe ereigniskorrelierter Potentiale (EKPs) zu prüfen.

In zwei Experimenten mit gleichem Wortmaterial wurden jeweils 20 Probanden in einer Lernphase 180 kategoriell geordnete Nomen dargeboten. Ein zeitlich verzögert präsentierter Hinweis zeigte an, ob das jeweilige Wort zu merken oder zu vergessen (Experiment 1) beziehungsweise tief oder flach (Experiment 2) zu verarbeiten war. In einem verzögerten Wiedererkennungstest mit Präsentation 180 neuer Wörter wurden die EKPs von 61 Skalpelektroden abgeleitet. Zentrale abhängige Variable waren alt/neu Effekte, das heißt die Differenz der durch richtige 'alt' und richtige 'neu' AntWörtern evozierten EKPs.

Die EKPs zeigten für richtig wiedererkannte Wörter verglichen mit richtig zurückgewiesenen neuen Wörtern mindestens drei topographisch und zeitlich verschiedene positive alt/neu Effekte mit frontomedianem, parietalem und rechtsfrontalem Maximum. Während sich diese EKP-Effekte als Funktion der Verarbeitungstiefe nur quantitativ unterschieden, gab es beim Wiedererkennen zu merkender und zu vergessender Wörter sowohl quantitative als auch qualitative Unterschiede zwischen den alt/neu Effekten. Insbesondere war bei zu vergessenden Items ein parietal verteilter alt/neu Effekt nicht nachweisbar und eine späte rechtsfrontale Positivierung stärker ausgeprägt. Ein Vergleich der beiden Experimente ergibt, daß die Annahme unterschiedlicher Verarbeitungstiefen für zu merkende und zu vergessende Wörter nicht zur Erklärung des intentionalen Vergessens genügt. Die Ergebnisse unterstützen vielmehr die Annahme, daß neben differentieller Enkodierung auch eine Hemmung des Gedächtnisabrufes erfolgt.

Abstract:

The decreased recognition performance for to-be-forgotten words in directed forgetting tasks is explained either by differential encoding or by inhibitory mechanisms at memory retrieval. The aim of the present study was to examine both explanatory models by means of event-related potentials (ERPs).

Two experiments using the same verbal stimulus material were performed with 20 participants each. In a study phase, they were presented with 180 nouns from the same categories. A delayed cue after each word instructed the participants whether they had to remember or forget the presented item (Experiment 1), or whether they had to process the item deeply or shallowly (Experiment 2). During a delayed recognition test the study words were presented along with 180 new words from the same categories, and ERPs were recorded from 61 scalp electrodes. The old/new effects, i.e. the difference of the ERPs elicited by correct 'old' and correct 'new' answers, were the central dependent variable.

The ERPs for correctly recognized words compared to correctly rejected new words showed at least three topographically and temporally different positive old/new effects with frontomedial, parietal and right frontal maxima. Whereas only quantitative differences as a function of depth of processing were found, quantitative as well as qualitative differences between old/new effects for to-be-remembered (TBR) and to-be-forgotten (TBF) words were revealed. In particular, the TBF items did not elicit any parietal old/new effect, but a larger late right frontal old/new effect than TBR items. A comparison of the spatio-temporal ERP patterns in both experiments revealed that differential encoding does not suffice for an explanation of intentional forgetting. The results provide support for the view that in addition to differential encoding also retrieval inhibition takes place, i.e. the TBF words are less accessible for retrieval processes.

Contents

CONTENTS

Contents

Acknowledgments

This dissertation was supported by a grant (Promotionsstipendium S 118) of the Gertrud Reemtsma Stiftung in der Max-Planck-Gesellschaft.

My supervisors Prof. Dr. D. Yves von Cramon, Prof. Dr. Axel Mecklinger, and Dr. Ulrich Müller have not only greatly supported my research but have also motivated me to pursue the interesting topic of this dissertation. Moreover, I would like to thank them for numerous fruitful discussions which helped me to develop own ideas.

Further, I wish to thank Anke Pitzmaus for her valuable assistance in generation of the stimulus material, to Joachim Wiese for his support in software production, and Ina Koch and Astrid Busch for their assistance in data collection.

Finally, I thank my father, Dr. Peter Ullsperger, who has aroused my interest in cognitive neurosciences in general and in event-related potential research in particular.

List of abbreviations

ANOVA	analysis of variance
BA	Brodman area
DC	direct current
EEG	electroencephalography
EOG	electrooculography
EPSP	excitatory postsynaptic potential
ERP	event-related potentials
Fig.	figure
IPSP	inhibitory postsynaptic potential
fMRI	functional magnetic resonance imaging
PET	positron emission tomography
R/K	remember/know
SME	subsequent memory effect
TBR	to-be-remembered
TBF	to-be-forgotten

All units of measurements are abbreviated according to the SI-System.

Chapter 1

Introduction

One of the most fundamental components of human cognition is memory. Memory has developed during evolution, it is the ability of living organisms to retain and utilize acquired information. Memory enables its owners to behave appropriately at a later time because of their experiences at an earlier time. Without a functioning memory, many other cognitive functions, such as reasoning, problem solving, planning, and language, would be impossible. Memory impairments (i.e., decreased ability to encode, store or retrieve information) have a strong impact on daily life and are an important medical and social problem, e.g., in patients with dementia. However, not only remembering but also forgetting - especially of irrelevant, potentially interfering information - is essential for a healthy memory and for goal-oriented actions.

People often understand forgetting as a failure of memory which is undesirable, and they wish to remember everything. However, do we really want to remember everything? Many people do not consider the negative consequences of never forgetting anything. There are events, such as the loss of a friend or embarrassing moments, which we do not want to remember. Moreover, it is conceivable that recalling currently irrelevant information can impair performance when pursuing a certain goal. For example, the performance of a short-order cook who during a typical breakfast shift must process many highly similar orders would suffer to the extent that the prior orders have not been forgotten (Bjork, 1970). There are many other situations when we need to forget in order to operate in a fast-changing environment: we need to remember our current telephone number and to forget our old one, or when leaving a shopping center we need to know where we have parked our car today and not yesterday. In other words, if we do not forget information which turned out to be wrong or no longer relevant, it will interfere with current, goal-relevant information. Being able to forget is as important to attaining performance goals as it is to be able to remember task-relevant information.

Not only memory researchers have long understood the importance and benefits of forgetting. Already in 1860, in his seminal *"Elemente der Psychophysik"* Gustav Theodor Fechner speculated about intentional manipulations of memories and forgetting:

*"...Die Hauptunterschiede zwischen den Nachbildern einerseits, Erinnerungs- und Phantasiebildern andererseits bestehen darin, dass die ersten stets nur mit einem Gefühle der Receptivität, nur in Continuität mit den gemachten sinnlichen Eindrücken, von Willkühr und Vorstellungsassociation unabhängig, entstehen und bestehen und nach Massgabe der unmittelbar vorhergegangenen sinnlichen Eindrücke auch von Willkühr unabhängig, gesetzlich, ablaufen, indess die Erinnerungs- und Phantasiebilder mit dem Gefühle geringerer oder grösserer Spontaneität noch längere Zeit nach vorausgegangenen sinnlichen Einwirkungen theils unwillkührlich durch Vorstellungsassociation entstehen, theils willkührlich hervorgerufen, wieder **verbannt** und abgeändert werden können." (Fechner, 1860, p. 469; bolding by the present author).*

In 1882 Ribot wrote that "forgetfulness, except in certain cases, is not a disease of memory, but a condition of its health and life". Another often cited statement by James (1890) says that "if we remembered everything, we should on most occasions be as ill off as if we remembered nothing." One of the major insights from directed forgetting research is how we deal with new information that renders old information irrelevant. The directed forgetting paradigm has been understood as a kind of model of memory updating.

The present study will investigate the mechanisms of intentional forgetting in healthy subjects using event-related brain potentials. This introductory chapter is divided into four sections. In Section 1.1, a short overview about the main concepts in modern memory research, which are of relevance for the present study, will be given. Current knowledge about intentional forgetting and models about the underlying mechanisms of this phenomenon will be outlined in Section 1.2. Section 1.3 discusses the method of event-related potential recording and its suitability for memory research. Finally, Section 1.4 summarizes the main questions and aims of the present study.

1.1 Main concepts in contemporary memory research: systems and processes

Processes of learning and memory are typically conceptualized as involving at least three stages: encoding, storage, and retrieval (e.g., Tulving, 1995). Encoding refers to acquisition of information. The idea is that encoding processes leave residues in the nervous system - memory traces - that persist over time. Thus, storage refers to maintaining information over time. The third stage, retrieval, means accessing stored information.

For the last decades, memory researchers have postulated that memory is not a unitary or monolithic entity, but is composed of several distinct but interacting component systems and processes (e.g., Tulving, 1995). This current understanding of the organization of human memory has evolved from various conceptual dichotomies: memory and habit, short-term and long-term memory, episodic and semantic memory etc. Evidence for distinct memory systems comes from behavioral dissociations in experimental psychology, studies of amnestic patients, and animal models (for overviews see, e.g., Squire & Knowlton, 1995; Squire & Zola, 1996; Tulving, 1995). The first comprehensive attempt to divide human memory into different systems was proposed by Atkinson and Shiffrin (1968). Their model postulated three broad sets of memory systems: sensory memory[1], short-term memory, and long-term memory. In the present study, long-term memory functions will be examined, therefore this short overview focuses on systems and processes in long-term memory. The most compelling evidence for a distinction between short-term memory and long-term memory comes from patients with anterograde amnesia. These patients often perform normally on immediate recall of short study lists (i.e., span tasks) as long as they are not distracted between study and test. Milner (1958) interpreted this syndrome as reflecting the inability to transfer information into long-term memory. She furthermore proposed that these patients must have intact short-term memory systems that work over distraction-free intervals. Short-term memory systems retain information for only a short time after it has been input or refreshed (rehearsed), and they have limited capacity. For a discussion of the short-term memory functions as a temporary storage for action-relevant information (which can be manipulated by a set of control processes) and as a selective window to the long-term memory systems, as well as for current working memory models the reader is referred to the literature (e.g., Atkinson & Shiffrin, 1968; Cowan, 1988; Cantor et al., 1991; Baddeley, 1995).

---

[1] Sensory channels (at least the auditory and visual ones) are equipped with sensory memory components which can hold a sensory trace of a stimulus over several hundreds of milliseconds or even seconds (Böttcher-Gandor & Ullsperger, 1992; Näätänen, 1992) after the stimulus offset. Traditionally, sensory memory systems are regarded as a way station in information processing (for an overview on sensory memory see Massaro & Loftus, 1996).

1.1.1 Long-term memory systems

Squire and colleagues (Squire & Knowlton, 1995; Squire & Zola, 1996) have proposed a taxonomy of long-term memory and related the systems to neuroanatomical structures (see Fig. 1.1). A very important distinction in human memory is that between declarative (explicit), and nondeclarative (implicit). Declarative memory refers to the conscious memory of facts (semantic memory) and events (episodic memory). Declarative memory is usually assessed by direct or explicit memory tests, such as free recall or recognition. In contrast, nondeclarative or implicit memory is revealed when previous experiences facilitate performance on a task that does not require conscious or intentional recollection of those experiences (Schacter, 1995). Typical forms of nondeclarative memory are, for example, priming, procedural memory (skills and habits), and classical conditioning. Priming refers to the increased ability to identify or detect a stimulus as a result of its recent presentation. Nondeclarative memory is typically tested with implicit or indirect memory tasks. A commonly used kind of tasks examining priming effects is word stem or word

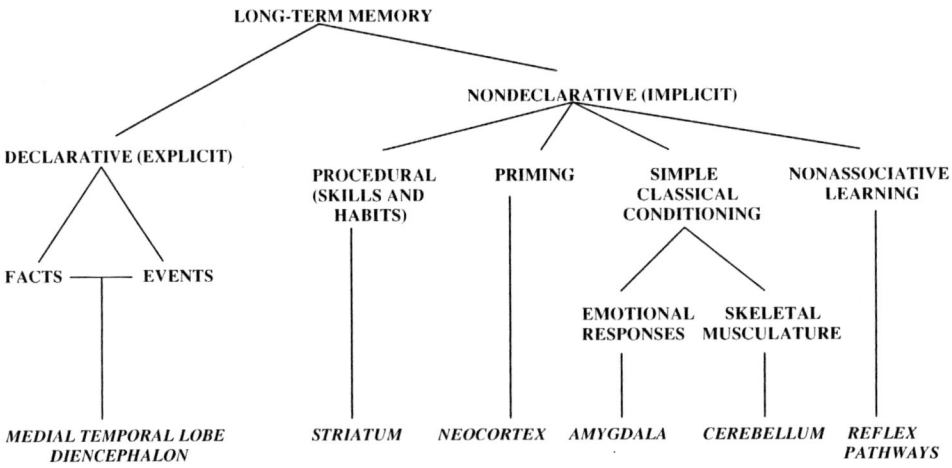

Figure 1.1 A taxonomy of long-term memory systems together with specific brain structures involved in each system (after Squire & Zola, 1996).

fragment completion. Usually, participants study a list of words (e.g. MOTEL) prior to the completion task. Subsequently, they are presented with word stems (e.g. MOT-), some of which belong to the studied words. The instructions are to complete each stem with the first word that comes to mind. Even when unaware of the relationship between study and test items, subjects are typically biased to complete stems with studied words rather then alternatives (e.g. MOTEL rather than MOTOR). Usually, responses to stems that are completed with study words are faster than to stems that have no relationship to the study list. However, it is important to note that stem completion tasks can be 'contaminated' by explicit memory for the studied lists (Schacter, 1997).

The present study investigates intentional forgetting in declarative, episodic memory employing a recognition test. Therefore, several special features of recognition memory should be mentioned. Recently, recognition memory has been commonly seen as a dual process (e.g., Jacoby & Kelley, 1992), determined both by the probability that an item is recognized on the basis of *conscious recollection* and on the basis of its *familiarity*. In other words, in recognition memory subjects experience two distinct states of awareness. Conscious recollection (also referred to as autonoetic awareness (e.g., Tulving, 1995; Düzel et al., 1997)) means that recognition of an item is accompanied by the retrieval of information about the context in which that item was last encountered, while familiarity (noetic awareness) refers to recognition judgments based on the feeling that an item has recently been encountered in the absence of any specific knowledge about the actual event (context) of its occurrence. These two kinds of recognition memory have been examined with the Remember/Know (R/K) procedure (Tulving, 1985). Recollection can clearly be identified as an example of explicit memory. However the place of familiarity based contributions to recognition memory within the explicit/implicit framework is less clear. A number of ERP studies has been performed to examine these models of recognition memory (e.g., Smith, 1993; Düzel et al., 1997; Rugg et al., 1998c). There has been observed an interesting dissociation between retrieval of an item and retrieval of the contextual information. While functioning of declarative memory depends on the integrity of the medial temporal lobe (including the hippocampus and the entorhinal, perirhinal, and the parahippocampal cortices) (Squire & Knowlton, 1995; Squire & Zola, 1996), successful retrieval of source and contextual information appears to additionally require intact frontal lobes (Shimamura, 1995).

5

1.1.2 Memory processes

As mentioned above, at least three distinct memory processes have been proposed: encoding, storage, and retrieval. An important issue in memory research concerns the relationship between how an item is processed at study (encoding) and its retrievability. The 'levels-of-processing' framework proposed by Craik and Lockhart (1972) assumes that the memorability (and strength of memory trace) increases as a function of the depth of encoding of an item. Items processed to the level of their physical features ('shallow encoding') are less likely to be remembered than those processed semantically ('deep encoding'). Phonological processing seems to have an intermediate position within this framework. Later on, the 'levels-of-processing' model has been criticized and subjected to revision (Craik & Tulving, 1975). However, the experimental manipulations acting on encoding reliably influence memory performance[2]. Therefore it has been repeatedly used as a tool in memory research using ERPs (e.g., Paller & Kutas, 1992; Rugg et al., 1998b). Manipulations of depth of encoding by influencing the mnemonic strategies (semantic or physical feature processing) were also applied to Experiment 2 of the present study in order to compare effects of directed forgetting with clearly encoding-related manipulations.

For the present study it is of high importance that the main memory processes can be influenced differentially. For example, damage of the hippocampal formation renders acquisition of new information difficult, whereas retrieval of information encoded prior to the damage seems to be less affected (Squire & Knowlton, 1995; Squire & Zola, 1996). Also psychological manipulations can affect encoding and retrieval differentially. The aforementioned levels-of-processing manipulation presumably acts on *encoding* strategies. In contrast, prior learning of some information can have influence on *retrieval* of similar material acquired later on: people are more likely to forget items from a list when a prior list has been studied. This phenomenon is called *proactive interference*. In other words, proactive interference refers to the negative effects that prior learning has on memory for more recently learned items. Proactive interference is assumed to act on retrieval processes (for a detailed

---

[2] It is important to note, however, that the levels of processing manipulation has no influence on implicit memory (Schacter & Graf, 1986).

discussion on current theories of proactive interference see Anderson & Neely, 1996). The present study examines the mechanisms underlying the intentional forgetting phenomenon, and an important question is whether and how intentional forgetting influences encoding or retrieval or both.

1.2 Intentional forgetting

1.2.1 Forgetting

Forgetting refers to the failure to remember previously encoded information. In short-term memory research it is common to assume that the activity trace naturally decays, whenever the trace is not actively maintained (e.g. Cowan, 1988; Baddeley, 1995). For long-term memory no entirely satisfying theory of forgetting has been put forward. It is still at issue whether forgotten information is permanently stored but inaccessible, or whether it has simply been lost from the memory system. Most researchers have favored the hypothesis of permanent storage, which is, however, problematic for its unfalsiability (for a detailed discussion of this issue see Eysenck & Kearne, 1990).

The present study investigates the mechanisms of intentional forgetting. As mentioned earlier, intentional forgetting is important for goal-directed behavior. It is conceivable that directed forgetting research is relevant for understanding how humans deal with irrelevant and interfering information. Moreover, it is important to note that the directed forgetting approach is one of the few established methods to directly examine processes involved in forgetting.

1.2.2 Review of intentional forgetting research

In recent decades a considerable amount of memory research has focused on the benefits of forgetting invalid or irrelevant information and on the possibility that forgetting can arise from intentional processes. Already in 1965, Muther employed a manipulation very similar to the directed forgetting method. Participants were presented several lists of 20 letters. They were told that for some lists all and for other lists only 10 letters had to be recalled. The 10 to-be-omitted (to-be-forgotten) letters were cued either before or after their presentation. When all 20 letters were to be recalled the correct recall accuracy was only 46 %, whereas from the cued lists 61 % were recalled correctly. Being allowed to omit half of the letters from recall resulted in significantly improved performance on the remaining ones. Despite this early evidence for separate mechanisms that enable intentional forgetting, it was not before 1968 that Bjork, LaBerge and Legrand (1968) really brought directed forgetting to the attention of memory researchers. In their study subjects were presented with 48 lists of digits, each of which also contained one or two target consonant strings. Subjects were instructed to name the digits and consonant targets, and then to recall them after each list. In some lists, subjects were cued just before the presentation of the second consonant string target that the first one could be forgotten. 39 % of the targets were recalled in lists with only one consonant string. In lists with two target strings, the specific directed forgetting pattern was observable: when both targets had to be remembered, only 15 % of second targets were recalled, whereas recall accuracy was about 30 %, when the first target could be forgotten. Bjork and colleagues concluded that directing or allowing subjects to forget the first item reduced the proactive interference on the second one, thus improving its recall. Following this seminal study, a considerable amount of experiments employing directed forgetting paradigms was performed.

1.2.2.1 The basic paradigms

A variety of procedures has been used to study the ability to forget some inputs while remembering others presented in the same context. A common feature of these directed forgetting procedures is that the cueing whether items are to be remembered (TBR) or to be forgotten (TBF) occurs after the items have been presented for study. There are two different methods of directed forgetting: First, the cueing whether an item has to be remembered or forgotten can occur after each item (single-item-cueing or item method), second, the cue is presented after a list of items has been studied and refers to all members of the previously studied list (blocked-cueing or list method). This distinction is important, because recent findings suggest that the item and list procedures invoke quite different processes, or at least a different weighting of the processing mechanisms that have been implicated in research on directed forgetting. Basden, Basden and Gargano (1993) thoroughly examined and compared both methods. They reported quite differing results for different kinds of manipulations between the two methods. A comprehensive comparison of the methods is also given in Basden and Basden (1998).

The two most basic, consistently observed findings in directed forgetting research are:

(1) a reduction of proactive interference from TBF items on subsequent material,

(2) a memory impairment for TBF items on a final memory test.

These findings were already reported in the study of Bjork, LaBerge and Legrand (1968) and replicated in dozens of later studies. Although several different models have been proposed to describe the mechanisms of directed forgetting, it is still at issue which processes are responsible for the directed forgetting effects, and whether the same processes are involved in different directed forgetting procedures. The most relevant models will briefly be outlined in the following chapter.

In directed forgetting research it is common to refer to a "directed-forgetting effect" as a measure of the effects of an instructional cue on memory performance. As noted by MacLeod (1998), this term has been used in different ways in the literature. To avoid confusion, in the present study the term "directed-forgetting effect" is used exclusively to describe the efficiency of intentional forgetting. Therefore, this term will be reserved for the difference of recognized TBR and recognized TBF words (TBR hits minus TBF hits).

1.2.2.2 Models of intentional forgetting: encoding operations versus retrieval operations

Current models (Anderson & Neely, 1996; H. M. Johnson, 1994; Zacks & Hasher, 1994) propose that multiple mechanisms underlie the effects of intentional forgetting, including

(1) differential encoding of TBR and TBF items, resulting from selective rehearsal of TBR items so that only these words are elaborately processed;

9

(2) segregation of TBR and TBF items into distinct sets in memory; and

(3) a repression-like process at the time of retrieval that prevents TBF items from being recovered. As a result, retrieval inhibition of TBF items occurs.

Thus, the first two processes should act on encoding of the presented items, whereas the last mechanism should act on the level of retrieval. Other possible explanations, such as active erasure of TBF items from short term memory, were not favored anymore, because already Muther (1965) had reported that TBF items appeared more often as intrusions than previously unpresented items, a finding which makes active erasure highly improbable.

Encoding operations

In the first years of directed forgetting research, Bjork and colleagues already proposed the *selective rehearsal model* (e.g., Bjork et al., 1968; Woodward & Bjork, 1971; Bjork, 1972), which explains many of the results in directed forgetting, especially when using the item method. The model assumes that TBF items do not receive the benefits of extended and elaborative rehearsal, consequently get a weaker memory trace, and are thus less accessible. It was argued that subjects used TBF cues in two ways: to segregate TBR from TBF items (set differentiation) and then to rehearse only TBR items (selective rehearsal). Several studies (Woodward and Bjork, 1971; Bjork & Woodward, 1973; Timmins, 1974; Wetzel, 1975; Wetzel & Hunt, 1977) examined the influence of the item-cue and the post-cue intervals on final recall and recognition. For TBF words the duration of the rehearsal interval prior to the cue had very little effect on final recall, but a beneficial effect on final recognition was found. Immediate cues favor TBR items because rehearsal and elaborate processing can begin right away, immediate cues correspondingly help to minimize TBF item acquisition. Wetzel (1975) combined directed forgetting with a levels-of-processing manipulation of encoding and found a difference in memory performance between TBR and TBF words in recall and recognition for both (deep and shallow) encoding conditions. Interestingly, the levels-of-processing manipulation affected TBR items only, i.e., only TBR words benefited from elaborate processing, while recall and recognition of TBF items was not significantly influenced by the levels of processing manipulation. It was argued that the forget cue stopped further processing of TBF words, a view consistent with the selective rehearsal account. Employing the remember/know procedure (Tulving, 1985), Gardiner et al. (1994) showed that the TBR item advantage in memory performance is largely in conscious recollection (more TBR than TBF items attracted the remember response, while the amount of know responses did not differ between TBR and TBF items), arguing that it is due to elaborate processing. Overall, selective rehearsal seems to be crucial in directed forgetting, especially in the item method.

Retrieval operations

However, there is converging evidence that at least part of the memory impairment observed in studies with directed forgetting using blocked-cueing methods results from a process that impairs access to items successfully encoded into long-term memory (Anderson & Neely, 1996). The first researchers to propose models of directed forgetting effects not only depending on encoding differences were Epstein with his selective search model and Weiner, the latter of whom related the directed forgetting effect to repression (Weiner, 1968; Weiner & Reed, 1969). Shebilske, Wilder and Epstein (1971) found that distraction-filled versus unfilled post-cue intervals had little impact on the size of the directed forgetting benefit. This is inconsistent with the selective rehearsal account, because filled intervals should prevent rehearsal. Although Epstein and colleagues (Epstein 1972; Epstein et al., 1972; Epstein & Wilder, 1972) considered that selective rehearsal also seemed to play a role, they strongly advocated the *selective search hypothesis*. They proposed that forget cues provide tags to differentiate items *at the time of retrieval*, permitting subjects to search only among the TBR items. This model was also supported by the result of a study, where syllable-word pairs had to be learned, showing that subjects rarely recalled a TBF item when they did not know that a TBF item was being tested, whereas their recall of TBF items improved dramatically when they knew that they had to recall a TBF word (Epstein & Wilder, 1972).

The idea of retrieval-related mechanisms of directed forgetting, later on referred to as the *retrieval inhibition* model, has been revived by Geiselman and colleagues about ten years later. Geiselman, Bjork, and Fishman (1983) provided support for the retrieval inhibition model using intentional and incidental encoding in the list paradigm of directed forgetting. Subjects heard a list of words and were told to learn one word and to judge the pleasantness of the next one, thus alternating intentional and incidental learning[3]. Half of the subjects were told to forget the preceding study words after half of the list was presented. It could be demonstrated that incidentally encoded words showed the same directed forgetting effects as intentionally encoded words, even though participants had no reason to rehearse the former items. These results indicated that impaired recall performance of TBF items is more than a failure to encode and rehearse those items to the same extent as TBR items. Furthermore, several findings argue that retrieval inhibition is also at least partly responsible for directed forgetting effects in studies employing *single-item-cueing* procedures. A very essential study of this kind was performed by Geiselman and Bagheri (1985). Subjects had to study 36 words, each followed by a remember or forget cue. As expected, participants recalled more TBR words (58 %) than TBF words (10 %). Thereafter they studied the same words again, but this time all words were to be remembered. Recall performance improved much more for the former TBF words (49 % recalled) than for the former TBR words (69 % recalled). Importantly, words not recalled on the first test were much more likely to be recalled on the second test if they had initially been TBF items (45 %) rather than TBR items (28 %). Geiselman and Bagheri argued that unrecalled TBF words benefited from a *release* from retrieval inhibition in addition to the extra rehearsal that both TBR and TBF items received. In other words, presenting unrecalled TBR and TBF items a second time as TBR words helped the TBF items more. The hypothesized inhibition of the access to the TBF words was disrupted by studying these items again with the instruction to remember.

Furthermore, MacLeod (1989) investigated the influence of directed forgetting on direct and indirect tests of memory. He noted that retrieval manipulations affect explicit and implicit memory in similar ways. In contrast, the degree of elaborative processing at encoding influences only direct memory tests (explicit memory), while performance in indirect memory tests is not improved by deep encoding (e.g., Schacter & Graf, 1986). The rationale of MacLeod's study was that if implicit and explicit memory was affected similarly by directed forgetting, this would support the notion that directed forgetting acts on retrieval processes rather than on encoding processes. MacLeod (1989) reported two experiments, each using one

---

[3] Incidental learning refers to tasks in which subjects are presented items without knowing that their memory for these items will be tested later in the experiment. Therefore, it can be assumed that participants do not rehearse or elaboratively process these items. In contrast, in intentional learning tasks subjects are instructed that they will be tested on the study items, therefore they are likely to employ high effort (extra rehearsal, deep processing) in encoding strategies.

direct and one indirect memory test after words had been studied in a single-item-cueing directed forgetting paradigm. In Experiment 1, the explicit recognition test showed a strong directed-forgetting effect (TBR: 69 %, TBF: 46 %). The implicit word fragment completion test revealed priming for both TBR (31 %) and TBF (24 %) items, and there was reliably more priming for TBR words. In Experiment 2, free recall (explicit memory) and repetition priming in a lexical decision task (implicit memory) were examined. Recall showed the typical directed-forgetting effect (TBR: 37 %, TBF 4 %), and lexical decision was also affected. Repetition priming was found for studied words: the subjects responded faster than to unstudied words (560 ms). Importantly, the responses to TBR words (523 ms) were even faster than to TBF words (540 ms). In summary, both implicit tests showed differential priming favoring TBR words, following the explicit test pattern. MacLeod's interpretation of these results was that both implicit and explicit memory were similarly affected by inhibition at the time of retrieval, consistent with the model of retrieval inhibition of Geiselman and colleagues (1983, 1985). However, MacLeod's results have repeatedly been challenged (Paller, 1990; Basden et al., 1993; H. M. Johnson, 1994; Hauselt, 1998). Paller (1990) as well as Basden et al. (1993) reported conflicting results. No directed forgetting effect on implicit tests such as word-stem completion was found. Paller (1990) suggested that the implicit tests used by MacLeod (fragment completion and lexical decision) may have been subject to explicit memory strategies, thereby transforming them into explicit tests, and this view was supported by Basden et al. (1993) and Hauselt (1998). Comparing the two directed forgetting procedures, Basden et al. (1993) noted that selective rehearsal may underlie the item method effects, whereas retrieval inhibition could explain the list method effects. This view is supported by the findings that the list method affects recall only, whereas in the item method recall and recognition are affected (Basden et al., 1993; MacLeod, 1998). Similarly, Wilson and Kipp (1998) argued that differential memory performance for TBF items in studies with single-item-cueing methods is due to selective rehearsal of TBR items only, hence they call this procedure "directed nonencoding" (p. 98) or "directed selective encoding" (p. 101).

Taking into account all evidence collected on the single-item-cueing method, differential encoding appears to be a crucial mechanism which can explain most phenomena of item method directed forgetting. However, some results (e.g., those of Geiselman & Bagheri, 1985) indicate that there could be involved additional mechanisms, such as retrieval inhibition. Therefore, the main question of the present study will be whether the underlying mechanisms of directed forgetting in the item method is really only differential encoding (as proposed by, e.g., Basden et. al., 1993, Basden & Basden, 1998, Wilson & Kipp, 1998), or whether differential encoding *and* retrieval inhibition are necessary for successful item-by-item directed forgetting.

As can be seen from this short overview, a considerable amount of work has been done to understand the psychological mechanisms underlying directed forgetting. Directed forgetting has been established as a tool in memory research, and it can be used as a model to investigate how the brain deals with irrelevant information. However, up to now only few studies addressed the neurobiological mechanisms involved in directed forgetting. Psychophysiological and neuroimaging studies could use the directed forgetting paradigms to investigate the physiological mechanisms of memory processes and the processing of irrelevant information. An interesting pharmacopsychological study has been performed by Müller and colleagues (Müller & Mecklinger, 1998; Müller, Mecklinger, & M. Ullsperger, in preparation) who examined the dopaminergic modulation of the directed forgetting effect. Several lines of evidence suggest that dopaminergic (D1) receptors in the prefrontal cortex are involved in inhibiting irrelevant information: Zacks, Radvansky, and Hasher (1996) have found a decline in directed forgetting effects in elderly adults, i.e., aged participants recalled less TBR and more TBF items, suggesting a less effective inhibition of irrelevant information. Taken together with the findings that D1-receptors in prefrontal cortex are diminished with aging and in schizophrenia (Iyo & Yamasaki, 1993; Okubo et al., 1997) these results could be a hint that dopaminergic activity in the prefrontal cortex helps to inhibit irrelevant information. Based on animal studies (Goldman-Rakic et al., 1997) and neuronal models of disturbances with dopaminergic dysfunctions (Cohen & Servan-Schreiber, 1992; Spitzer, 1997) Müller and colleagues assumed that the dopaminergic receptors in the prefrontal cortex modulate the inhibition of irrelevant information. Thus, based on the retrieval inhibition model of directed forgetting Müller et al. predicted that an D1-Agonist would enhance the efficiency of intentional forgetting. Two within-subject double-blind placebo-controlled experiments were performed. In the first experiment, subjects performed a directed forgetting task after administration of pergolide (a D1/D2 agonist) or placebo. To control for possible ceiling effects, another group of participants performed the same experiment after pretreatment with the dopamine antagonist sulpiride. That is, they either took pergolide or placebo after pretreatment with sulpiride. The clearest results were obtained, when conscious recollection (tested with the Remember/Know procedure introduced by Tulving (1985)) was examined. While there were only minimal, nonsignificant changes in recollection rates of TBR words, indicating that encoding and retrieval mechanisms were not much influenced by the pharmacological manipulation, there were differences in recollection rates of TBF words depending on whether pergolide was applicated or not. In the experiment without pretreatment, pergolide led to higher recollection rates of TBF words. This was a quite surprising result, because in contrast to the prediction it indicated that a stimulation of D1-receptors diminished the inhibition of TBF items, i.e., the efficiency of intentional forgetting was decreased. The results of the second experiment were also very interesting: when subjects were pretreated with the dopamine antagonist sulpiride, recollection of TBF items was also enhanced (placebo session). Subsequent intake of pergolide lowered the recollection rate of TBF items almost back to the level, which was measured in the placebo session without pretreatment. In other words, both the intake of a dopamine agonist as well as of an antagonist enhanced recollection of TBF items and thus lowered the directed forgetting effect. Moreover, the diminished directed forgetting effect after application of the dopamine antagonist could be raised again by application of a dopamine agonist. The main results are displayed in Fig. 1.2.

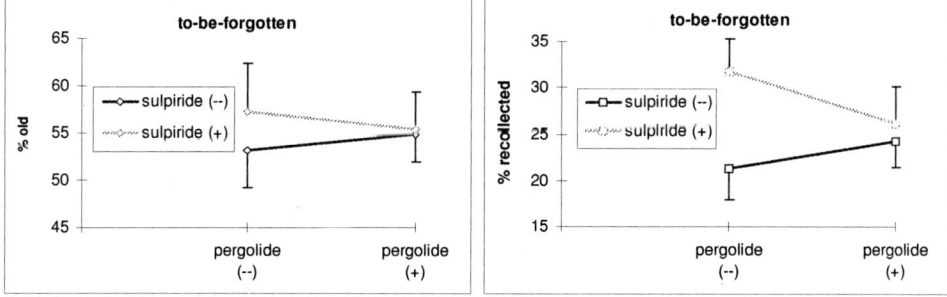

Figure 1.2 Influence of the dopamine agonist pergolide on recognition (left graph) and conscious recollection (right graph) rates of TBF words in a directed forgetting paradigm with and without pretreatment with the dopamine antagonist sulpiride.

These seemingly contradicting results can be interpreted in a model hypothesizing an inverted u-shaped optimum curve of dopamine activity. In normal subjects the dopamine level at prefrontal cortical receptors should be optimal, enabling subjects to inhibit most irrelevant information. However, when the dopaminergic activity deviates from the optimum (e.g., after intake of a drug acting on dopamine receptors), the inhibition of TBF words should be suboptimal. This hypothesis has to be further evaluated in experiments with patients who have a dopaminergic dysfunction, such as schizophrenia. Studies using pharmacological manipulations combined with psychophysiological measures will surely contribute to the understanding not only of directed forgetting but also of more general cognitive mechanisms, e.g., inhibition. However, pharmacological studies have some methodological drawbacks: first, especially in patient studies it is difficult to use a double-blind placebo-controlled study design, second, the measured effects are often low and require large patient groups, and third, many drugs are not specific to one kind of receptor, making interpretations very difficult. Moreover, in the aforementioned directed forgetting paradigm used by Müller and colleagues it cannot be distinguished whether pharmacological intervention acts on encoding, retrieval or both. Therefore, it makes sense to investigate memory processes with psychophysiological methods, such as event-related potential recordings, which have a high temporal resolution and allow a process specific analysis. The present study employs a paradigm very similar to that used by Müller et al. In this study, electrophysiological changes related to processes involved in directed forgetting will be examined in order to add another piece to the puzzle. The next chapter will describe the use of even-related potentials as a method well suited for examination of cognitive processes.

1.3 Event-related potentials and memory research

1.3.1 Event-related brain potentials - a powerful tool in cognitive neuroscience

Event-related brain potentials (ERPs) are small voltage oscillations recorded by means of electrodes at the scalp, and they reflect electrical activity of the brain time-locked to the ongoing information processing of a particular event, such as the presentation of a stimulus or a (re)action of the subject (Hillyard & Kutas, 1983).

ERPs, their generation and functional significance, have been under intensive and very productive investigation for more than three decades. As noted by Coles (1989), ERPs have a dual status. They allow to investigate physiological as well as psychological processes, or "they can serve as ... 'windows' on cognition - and they can serve as ... 'windows' on the brain" [p. 251]. The ERP approach can be used as a link between neuroscience and cognitive psychology, it is a valuable method to investigate functionally relevant brain activity. ERP studies of cognitive processes far outnumber those conducted with other psychophysiological techniques. The relative maturity of the ERP field has led to a substantial degree of consensus about the methodological standards. Hence, application of ERP methods can answer questions about the neurophysiology of the brain and about cognitive functions with high reliability. Moreover, it can be used for investigation of pathological states. In this section the electrophysiological basis of ERPs, some methodological aspects of data acquisition and processing, and drawing inferences about cognitive functions from ERP data will be discussed. In Section 1.3.2, ERP correlates of memory functions relevant for the present study will be reviewed.

1.3.1.1 The generation of ERPs

Although it is generally accepted that ERPs reflect electrical activity originating in the brain, the exact biophysical relationship between the neurophysiological processes taking place in the brain and the potential changes which we observe at the scalp is not completely understood (for detailed discussions of the physiological determinants of the ERP waveform see Nunez, 1981; and Wood, 1987). ERPs represent electrical fields associated with the synchronized activity of a sizable population of neurons which have a certain geometric configuration. The neurons must be arranged in such a way that their individual electrical fields summate to yield a dipolar field, usually this is the case when the neurons are aligned in a parallel orientation (open fields). If the configuration of individual neurons does not allow such a summation of electrical fields (closed fields) or the activity of the neurons is not sufficiently synchronized, no electrical field will be detectable at the scalp. In some brain structures, such as the neocortex, neuronal populations of a sufficient size with neurons that share the same orientation (perpendicular to the scalp surface) are likely to produce synchronized electrical activity, which is volume-conducted to the scalp. However, in other structures, such as the thalamus, the configuration of the neurons prevent a sufficient summation and propagation of electrical fields, such that activity of these neurons will be 'invisible' at the scalp. This consideration implies that, first, a considerable amount of brain activity cannot be detected at the surface of the head and, second, the most important generators of ERP components with high amplitudes should be located in cortical (and sometimes partly subcortical) structures (cf. Nunez, 1981; Rugg & Coles, 1995; Kutas & Dale, 1997).

Biophysical and neurophysiological considerations suggest that ERP waveforms result from a modulation of dendritic inhibitory or excitatory postsynaptic potentials (IPSP and EPSP, respectively), whereas axonal action potentials do not seem to play a role in the generation of ERPs (Allison et al., 1986; Birbaumer et al., 1990). Particularly for slow potential changes[4] it was argued, that the generating structures are located below the recording site (Somjen, 1973; Lang et al., 1988). Homan et al. (1987), Lagerlund et al. (1993) and Towle et al. (1993) established a correspondence between electrode site and underlying cerebral structure using radiographic or magnetic resonance imaging techniques. The results reported by Homan et al. (1987) are displayed in Table 1.1. They can be useful for identification of cortical sources especially of slow potentials. However, volume conduction mostly prevents an exact determination of ERP generators (see also next section).

---

[4] Slow potentials are those ERP deflections which can be observed in the vicinity of an eliciting stimulus or event and may sustain for several seconds. For an overview cf. McCallum & Curry (1993).

Table 1.1 Localization of the scalp electrodes of the 10-20 system according to Homan et al. (1987)

Electrode position	Brodman area	Cortical structures
Fp1, Fp2	10	rostral margin of the superior frontal gyrus
F3, F4	46	middle frontal gyrus, near superior frontal sulcus
F7 F8	45 46	inferior frontal gyrus, rostral portion of pars triangularis
C3, C4	4	precentral gyrus (shoulder to wrist area), middle frontal gyrus
P3, P4	7	superior parietal lobule near intraparietal sulcus, superior to posterior portion of supramarginal gyrus
TP3, TP4	40	inferior parietal lobule, anterior portion of supramarginal gyrus
T1, T2	38	temporal pole overlapping superior temporal sulcus, more middle than superior temporal gyrus
T3 T4	21 22	middle and superior temporal gyri, posterior to central sulcus
T5 T6	37 19, 37, 39	middle temporal gyrus, caudal to termination of Sylvian fissure superior temporal sulcus, termination of Sylvian fissure
O1, O2	17	occipital lobe, lateral and superior to occipital pole, overlapping calcarine fissure

1.3.1.2 Data acquisition and processing

ERPs represent stimulus-locked electrical activity embedded in the electroencephalogram (EEG), which is recorded as the difference in voltage between two electrode sites. This is achieved by attaching several explorative electrodes to scalp localizations of interest and a reference electrode to a place, which should be relatively uninfluenced by the electrical activity of interest, and connecting these electrodes to a differential amplifier.

In most cases, the amplitude of the ERP is very small (microvolts) in relation to the EEG waveform (tens of microvolts). Thus, the stimulus-locked ERP activity must be extracted from the background EEG by averaging techniques. This averaging method is based on the assumption that event-related activity is time-locked to a specific event, whereas the background EEG activity fluctuates randomly. Thus, a number of EEG epochs, each of which is time-locked to repetitions of the same event. Averaging of the digital values of these EEG epochs will lead to an elimination of randomly varying background EEG and an isolation of the event-related activity (for a detailed discussion of the ERP methodology and averaging techniques see, e.g., Coles, Gratton, Kramer & Miller, 1986, and Regan, 1989, pp. 47-57).

Averaging techniques alone are sometimes not sufficient to control for all artifactual electrical activity which arises from sources other than the brain. High-frequency activity attributable to muscle activity and line frequency (e.g., 50 Hz) can be attenuated by low-pass filtering of the signal, whereas low frequency activity, such as DC drifts, can be dealt with using a high-pass filter with a very low cut-off frequency or by applying a detrending procedure (Regarding possible distortions of the waveform by filtering cf. Regan, 1989, pp. 8-33). However, two major sources of artifacts, movements of the eyes and eyelids, cannot be dealt with in that way, because these movements occur at the same frequencies as important features of the ERP waveforms. Therefore, in many experiments subjects are instructed to maintain their gaze at a fixation point and to avoid blinking. Moreover, the experimenter may discard all EEG epochs contaminated with activity caused by eye blinks or movements. The problem here is that there may result an insufficient number of artifact-free trials to allow the extraction of a reliable ERP waveform by averaging. Some investigators have therefore developed procedures that estimate and remove the contribution of eye movements and blinks to the ERP signal (e.g., Gratton et al., 1983; Pfeifer, 1993; for a recent comparison of correction methods see Gratton, 1998).

The ERP is characterized by a sequence of negative and positive deflections of voltage in the time domain. These deflections can be described by their latency relative to the event of interest, their polarity, and their amplitude relative to the baseline. The baseline is usually defined as the mean voltage level for some time periods which should not be influenced by the stimulus (often preceding the stimulus). Traditionally, the deflections of the ERP waveforms are described as components defined by typical polarity, minimal peak latency, and topographical scalp distribution. After defining interesting ERP components in such a way, changes of amplitude and latency can be measured when experimental variables are manipulated. This straightforward approach, however, can be problematic. The waveform observed at the scalp results from the summation of electrical activity that may be generated by different sources in the brain. Volume conduction by the brain tissue, meninges, skull, and scalp (Nunez, 1981) can propagate activity such that it can be detected at distant locations. Thus, it is conceivable that a voltage change detected at a certain recording site can be attributable to overlapping activity of a variety of different generators at different locations. Moreover, there need be no direct correspondence between the timing of a deflection and the temporal characteristics of the underlying neural structures (Coles & Rugg, 1995; Gevins & Cutillo, 1993). Because of those ambiguities, several researchers have used two more complex approaches to definition of ERP components. The *physiological approach* postulates that only those parts of an ERP which can be unequivocally related to one neuronal generator can be defined as a component (Näätänen & Picton, 1987). For source identification a variety of methods has been used, e.g., intracranial recordings (e.g., Halgren et al. 1980, 1995), lesion studies (e.g., Knight, 1990, 1997; Rugg, 1992; Mecklinger et al., 1998), the application of functional neuroimaging methods (e.g., Opitz et al., 1999), and dipole localization techniques (e.g., Scherg & von Cramon, 1986; Mecklinger & Ullsperger, 1996; Hegerl & Frodl-Bauch, 1997).

The *psychological approach* defines a component as a correlate of cognitive functions. In other words, this interpretation allows a functional identification of components also in cases, when multiple generators contribute to a certain ERP pattern, provided that these generators form a functionally homogenous system. One way to cope with the component overlap and to isolate components whose presence differentiates between experimental conditions is to subtract the ERPs for those conditions (cf. Coles & Rugg, 1995; Hoormann et al., 1998). Whatever is different between the two waveforms will form the component of interest, which is then identified as an ERP correlate of whatever cognitive process is believed to differ between the conditions. One has to be aware, however, that application of this subtraction method can lead to a misinterpretation of latency differences as amplitude differences (Coles & Rugg, 1995).

In the following, ERP components being of relevance for the investigation of memory processes will be reviewed (Section 1.3.2). Prior to this I will turn to the general conceptual question how one can draw inferences from ERP data about the reflected cognitive processes.

1.3.1.3 Inferences from ERP data

In contrast to other physiological measures of brain activity, which are based on, e.g., the hemodynamic response of the cerebral vascular system (fMRI, PET), ERPs detect brain activity with virtually unlimited temporal resolution. Furthermore, synchronized activity in properly oriented neuronal populations of only several tens of milliseconds is sufficient to be registered at the scalp (Kutas & Dale, 1997; Kutas & Federmeier, 1998).

Differences in timing and scalp topographies of particular ERP components can be used to make inferences about the timing and the spatial configuration of brain activity involved in cognitive processes (e.g., R. Johnson, 1993; Rugg & Coles, 1995). On the basis of their high temporal resolution ERPs are very suitable for distinguishing the subprocesses underlying different cognitive functions, such as retrieval operations, by appropriate separations along the time dimension (time windows).

For interpretation of ERP findings also comparison of topographical scalp distributions of the observed components under different experimental conditions can be helpful. It is important to note that topographical differences of ERP effects can only occur if their neural generators differ with respect to their localization. By contrast, ERP effects that differ in their magnitude but are topographically equivalent indicate that the respective experimental conditions engaged the same population of generators, with different strengths of activation (R. Johnson, 1993). Hence, ERP effects differing only in magnitude reflect different levels of engagement of the same neurophysiological processes, whereas a difference in scalp topography is highly suggestive that the cognitive processes engaged in the respective experimental conditions are at least partially functionally dissociable (Rugg & Coles, 1995).

These considerations implicate that for differentiation of cognitive operations by means of ERPs clear models and hypotheses are necessary. Both aspects of ERP research - the identification of their cognitive correlates and their neural origins - have already made a significant contribution in cognitive neuroscience (cf. e.g., Rugg and Coles, 1995; Kutas & Dale, 1997).

1.3.2 Event-related potential correlates of memory processes

Many ERP components have a systematic relationship to memory processes, broadly defined (Kutas, 1988). For example, several ERP components, such as the mismatch negativity, are sensitive to stimulus probability, a property which suggests that these components reflect some elementary memory representations. However, this section aims to discuss only those ERP components which seem to be specifically related to encoding and retrieval of information in long-term memory, and which are, therefore, of high relevance for the present study.

1.3.2.1 ERP studies of encoding

In the last two decades numerous studies have investigated ERP phenomena related to memory encoding. Most of these studies have used variations of a single paradigm, in which in a study task a series of items is presented while EEG epochs time-locked to the presentation of each item are recorded. Subsequently, memory for these items is tested. The EEG data registered at study is then used to form two classes of ERPs, associated respectively with successfully and unsuccessfully retrieved items. Differences of the ERPs at study as a function of the subsequent memory performance are referred to as "Dm" (difference due to memory, Paller et al., 1987a) or subsequent memory effects (SME). The latter term was introduced by Rugg & Coles (1995), because Dm - although originally intended to be purely descriptive - can easily be misunderstood as a single component or mechanism with a causal role in memory encoding. The first study which described these SME was performed by Sanquist et al. (1980), who found at study a more positive-going waveform of ERPs for words which had been subsequently successfully recognized compared with the ERPs for unrecognized words. These findings have been replicated and extended in many studies performed by several groups of researchers.

In a series of studies, Donchin, Fabiani, and colleagues investigated the relationship between ERPs elicited by words at study and the words' subsequent retrievability employing the 'von Restorff' (von Restorff, 1933) procedure (Karis et al., 1984; Fabiani et al., 1990; Donchin & Fabiani, 1991; Fabiani & Donchin, 1995). In this procedure, sequences of items are presented, some of which (so called 'von Restorff' events) deviate in some way from the others (e.g., by different letter size). Memory performance for those deviant items is usually better than for other members of the study list. Karis et al. (1984) segregated the subjects post hoc into two groups with either large or small 'von Restorff' index (a measure of the relative recall advantage of 'von Restorff' items). Interestingly, the subjects with large indices reported adopting rote mnemonic strategies, such as permanent rehearsal, whereas subjects with low indices reported the use of elaborative strategies, such as association of a study item with stories or pictures). Although in both groups more positive-going ERPs to subsequently retrieved items were found, these SMEs differed between the two groups. Karis et al. (1984) argued that in the subjects adopting a rote strategy the SME resulted from the modulation of a parietal-maximum P300 component, whereas in elaborators a later SME was observed at the frontal electrode. In a later study, Fabiani et al. (1990) directly manipulated mnemonic strategies. The results of the former study could be replicated. Donchin and Fabiani (1991) argued that these different SME reflect functionally dissociable processes: elaborative processing (e.g., inter-item associations) is reflected during encoding is reflected by a positive, late frontal slow potential. In contrast, SME in the time window of the P300 component should reflect variations in distinctiveness of the events.

Other groups could show, that SME are not only observable for somehow deviating, rare events. Neville et al. (1986) argued that the SME reflects the amount of elaborative encoding of presented words. Paller and associates have reported several studies of ERPs and memory encoding. In the first study (Paller et al., 1987a), they employed an incidental memory task which varied the level of processing. The SME was found in all tasks but was larger for those requiring semantic processing. Interestingly, they also reported an amplitude difference between two different semantic tasks. Thus, Paller et al. argued that SME did not merely reflect the extent of semantic processing. In a following study Paller et al. (1988) reported a difference of the SME in two direct memory tasks, recognition and recall; SME were larger for the recall task. In two studies (Paller et al., 1987b; Paller, 1990) examining the

24

SME in direct and indirect memory tests the group found discrepant ERP results. While in the former study ERPs at study phase averaged according to performance in a stem completion test showed an SME, such a difference was not found in the second study. Paller (1990) argued that in the former study the stem completion performance was much higher due to a 'contamination' by explicit memory. Further he interpreted the findings as evidence that explicit and implicit memory rely on qualitatively different encoding processes[5].

Mecklinger and Müller (1996) performed a study-test procedure in which subjects had to remember either simple geometric objects irrespective of their position in a 4 by 4 spatial matrix (object memory task) or spatial positions of the objects irrespective of their forms (spatial memory task). In the object task they found an SME to which the P300 and a frontally located slow wave following P300 contributed. However, in the spatial memory task, no ERP difference was found between positions remembered and not remembered later. The authors argued that the absence of an SME could be due to less elaborated mnemonic strategies used in the spatial task.

Although the above cited studies differ in terms of the stimulus material and the memory tests, it was shown, that ERPs at encoding covary with the subsequent memory performance for the encoded items. Recently, similar findings were reported in studies using functional MRI: activations in frontal cortex and mediobasal temporal cortex predicted which presented items were later remembered and which were not remembered (Brewer et al., 1998; Wagner et al., 1998b; Fernández et al., 1998). In future, integration of ERP and fMRI findings will certainly lead to a more comprehensive understanding of neural processes involved in memory encoding.

1.3.2.2 Retrieval processes

ERP associated with retrieval operations have been examined in a wide variety of studies. This section will consider recognition-related ERP phenomena, because in the present study ERPs recorded during recognition tests were investigated. For a detailed discussion of ERP repetition effects in indirect memory tests see Rugg (1995). A consistent finding in ERP

---

[5] However, there were several objections against this view, and alternative interpretations were suggested (e.g., Rugg, 1995).

studies of recognition memory is that correctly recognized old stimuli evoke more positive-going waveforms than do correctly recognized new stimuli. This difference - commonly referred to as the old/new effect - starts around 300 ms post stimulus and persists several hundred milliseconds (cf. Rugg, 1995; R. Johnson, 1995; Johnson et al., 1998). Based on temporal and topographical distributions, several subcomponents of the old/new differences have been distinguished. In other words, the old/new effect consists of at least three spatially separate but temporally overlapping subcomponents.

An *early frontal old/new effect* starting at approximately 300 ms post stimulus and lasting around 200 ms has been observed in a variety of studies (e.g., R. Johnson et al., 1998; Mecklinger, 1998; Mecklinger & Meinshausen, 1998; Rugg et al., 1998b, 1998c). Johnson et al. (1998) noted that the early frontal old/new effect is important because it is the first electrophysiological sign known to discriminate old from new information. It was proposed that it reflects in part a modulation of a negative component, i.e., old words elicit less negativity than new words which leads to a positive difference over frontal scalp in the difference waveforms. The amplitude maximum of this old/new effect is located at frontal midline recording sites, and it has been suggested to be associated with familiarity during recognition judgments presumably resulting from facilitated access to conceptual and/or lexical information. The latter notion has been supported by the findings of a combined ERP and fMRI study examining false memories (Mecklinger et al., 1999, and personal communication). They argued that a medial to right frontal negative component at around 350 ms is elicited by memory search processes. This negative component is most pronounced in trials where new words that are semantically associated with old words have been correctly rejected. Interestingly, the fMRI experiment performed with the same task and stimulus material revealed increased activity in the right inferior frontal gyrus for the same experimental condition. The reaction time data suggested that for those words the memory scanning has been most intensively performed. For correctly recognized words as well as for semantically related words that were erroneously classified as old this negative wave was largely attenuated. Mecklinger et al. argued that familiarity as well as illusionary familiarity (as for erroneously classified semantically related items) could have stopped or at least diminished memory scanning processes resulting in the early frontal positive old/new difference. Thus, the early frontal old/new effect could be a correlate of familiarity (Rugg et al., 1998b; Mecklinger et al., 1999; Penney et al., 1999).

The *parietal old/new effect* has been described as a positive-going deflection which onsets approximately 400 ms post stimulus, lasts several hundred milliseconds, and is largest over parietal and temporal regions of the scalp. For verbal material the effect usually is lateralized to the left hemisphere. Several lines of evidence indicate that the parietal old/new effect is associated with conscious recollection (for a review cf. Allan et al., 1998). Early findings in support of this idea were reported by Smith (1993). He employed the Remember/Know (R/K) procedure (Tulving, 1985) to dissociate recollection and familiarity based recognition judgments. In this procedure subjects were required to make a second introspective judgment in case they have recognized an item. They were told to signal whether they "remembered" the test item because recognition was accompanied by a "recollective experience" (i.e., they could remember details of the study episode), or whether they merely "knew" that it was old because it felt familiar. Smith (1993) found that old/new effects were almost twice as large for recognized items associated with remember responses as for those associated with know responses. It was argued that the parietal old/new effect reflects conscious recollection (but see also Spencer et al., 1994, for a different interpretation).

In a series of studies, Rugg and colleagues employed a source memory procedure to compare ERPs associated with recognition memory judgments which differed in their likelihood of being based on recollection (Wilding et al., 1995, Wilding & Rugg, 1996, 1997). In their experiments they separated ERPs elicited by correctly recognized old items according to the accuracy of a subsequent source judgment. Trials on which source memory was successful would be more likely to include recollection of details of the study episode than for trials on which the source judgment was unsuccessful. In these latter trials recognition judgments would therefore be based more often solely on familiarity. In all studies the ERPs evoked by words attracting incorrect source judgments were associated with effects qualitatively similar to those elicited by correct source judgments, but smaller in magnitude. In a follow up study, Wilding and Rugg (1997) investigated old/new effects in a recognition memory exclusion task similar to that employed by Yonelinas and Jacoby (1994). In this study, subjects performed an encoding task in which words were spoken in either male or female voices. In the recognition memory test, subjects were instructed to respond on one key to studied words that had been spoken in one of the two voices (target, included) and on another key both to old words spoken in the second voice (non-targets, excluded) and to new words. The ability to merely discriminate between old and new, i.e., recognition based solely on familiarity, will not suffice to permit accurate performance. Misclassification of non-targets should hence be due to a combination of recollection failure and high familiarity. The correctly classified targets and non-targets elicited reliable parietal effects. In my opinion, one of the most important findings is that misclassified non-targets (items with high familiarity but recollection failure) did not evoke a parietal old/new effect. Taken together, the findings give clear support to the proposal that the left parietal effect is associated with conscious recollection and not with familiarity.

In a next step, Rugg et al. (1998c) addressed the question whether source judgments and the Remember/Know procedure define recollection in the same way. In the R/K task they found the same old/new effects, topographically indistinguishable from those in the source task. This was interpreted as support for the view that recollection defined by accurate source discrimination and recollection defined by subjective experience are neurally and functionally equivalent. Based on results of a combined ERP and PET study, Rugg et al. (1998d) speculates about the possible generators of the recollection-related parietal old/new effect. It seems very improbable that the parietal old/new effect directly reflects the involvement of the hippocampal formation in episodic retrieval due to the anatomical structure suggesting that neurons of this structure form a closed field. A more plausible interpretation by Rugg et al. suggests that this effect reflects changes in cortical activity resulting from cortico-hippocampal interactions, that have been proposed to underlie episodic memory retrieval (McClelland et al., 1995).

Also other groups (e.g., Paller et al., 1995; Düzel et al., 1997; Johnson et al., 1998) agree that the parietal old/new effect is associated with conscious recollection. Moreover, Johnson and colleagues (Johnson, 1995; Johnson et al., 1998) suggested that the parietal old/new effect is overlapped by an independent modulation of the P300 component which may reflect the strength or accessibility of the memory trace.

Finally, the *right frontal old/new effect* is an ERP modulation with an amplitude maximum over the right frontal scalp. It onsets at a similar or slightly longer latency as the parietal effect, but it is considerably more sustained in time. The right frontal effect was hypothesized to be associated with post-retrieval operations necessary to reconstruct and maintain information from the study episode (Allan et al., 1998; Wilding & Rugg, 1996). For example, in the source memory study reported by Wilding & Rugg (1996) items attracting successful source jugdments elicited the late right frontal old/new effect, which was attenuated for recognized items with incorrect source memory. A later study (Rugg et al., 1998c) replicated this finding for source memory and R/K jugdments. A similar right frontal old/new effect was also described by Mecklinger who examined recognition memory for object form and spatial location (Mecklinger, 1998; Mecklinger & Meinshausen, 1998).

It was suggested that the late right frontal old/new effect reflects neural activity originating from right prefrontal cortex, and in its functional and spatial characteristics it resembles recent results from PET and fMRI data on memory retrieval (e.g., Wilding & Rugg, 1996; Rugg et al., 1998a). This explanation is plausible because retrieval of contextual information and processes that operate on the retrieved information are known to depend on frontal lobe function (Stuss et al., 1994; Moscovitch, 1992; Schacter, 1987; Shimamura & Squire, 1987; Shimamura, 1995). It is important to note, however, that so far there is no consensus on the functional significance of right prefrontal activations in PET and fMRI studies on explicit memory retrieval tasks (cf. Wagner et al., 1998a), nor it is completely understood whether or not the right frontal old/new ERP effect and brain metabolic changes in the right prefrontal cortex reflect the same processing function.

1.4 The aim of the present study

The aim of the present study was to examine the issue of whether lower recognition of TBF items in a single-item-cueing directed forgetting paradigm is caused by differential encoding alone, or whether additional processes such as retrieval inhibition contribute to the lower memory performance of TBF items. This was achieved by comparing event-related brain potentials in recognition memory tests for TBR and TBF words (Experiment 1) and for words that had undergone either deep and shallow encoding (Experiment 2). The aims of this investigation were to:

(1) investigate ERP correlates of encoding in the directed forgetting paradigm,

(2) isolate ERP correlates of retrieval processes necessary for recognition of verbal material which has undergone either a directed forgetting procedure or a depth of encoding manipulation,

(3) compare the spatio-temporal pattern of recognition-related ERPs recorded in both experiments and

(4) make inferences about the cognitive processes involved in directed forgetting.

The rationale of the latter point was as follows: In the foregoing chapter it was pointed out that different spatio-temporal ERP patterns can be attributed to different cognitive subprocesses. Given that the differential memory performance in item-by-item directed forgetting is a result of differential encoding alone, the spatio-temporal patterns of the old/new effects obtained in both experiment should not differ. In contrast, differences in ERP patterns between both experiments would suggest, that at least partially differential cognitive processes are involved in word recognition in a directed forgetting paradigm compared to a depth of encoding manipulation.

More specific hypotheses will be formulated in Chapter 3 after the description of Methods and Materials.

Chapter 2

Methods and Materials

2.1 Experiment 1 - ERP study of intentional forgetting

2.1.1 Participants

Twenty volunteers (11 female) between 20 and 31 years of age (mean: 23.5 years) participated in this experiment. All participants were students at the University of Leipzig. They reported to be in good health and had normal or corrected-to-normal vision and gave written informed consent prior to the experiment. For their participation they were paid 13 DM per hour. None of the participants had any prior experience with the task.

2.1.2 Stimuli

All stimuli were presented in central vision on a 17" VGA monitor under the control of a Pentium computer. Stimuli consisted of 360 German nouns taken from a categorized word pool, which was created in a categorial noun generation experiment previously performed with 139 undergraduate students at the University of Leipzig (107 female, mean age 22.2 (18 - 34) years). The verbal material is displayed in the Appendix. There were 36 categories and the mean word typicality of the 10 category examples was matched across categories. The words were arranged into 6 study lists, such that each list was 30 words long and contained 5 members from 6 categories. In addition, the 6 categories in each list differed in their assignment to to-be-remembered words and to-be-forgotten words such that they contained 0 TBR words and 5 TBF words (0R:5F), 1 TBR word and 4 TBF words (1R:4F), 2 TBR words and 3 TBF words (2R:3F), 3 TBR words and 2 TBF words (3R:2F), 4 TBR words and 1 TBF word (4R:1F), and 5 TBR words and 0 TBF words (5R:0F), respectively (cf. Zacks et al., 1996). The remaining 5 nouns from each category were not presented in the study phase but were used as new words in the test phase. In each study list the order of items was pseudo-randomized so that TBR and TBF words were equally distributed in the first and second half of the list, not more than 3 TBR or TBF items were presented consecutively, and the first and last TBF item was from a different category. Subject to these constraints, 4 sets of study lists were generated, across which the assignment of TBR, TBF, and new items to the categories were counterbalanced. Each set of lists was used for the same number of participants. In the recognition test all 360 words were presented in randomized order.

2.1.3 Procedure

The participants sat comfortably in an acoustically and electrically shielded dimly lit chamber at a distance of about 90 cm from the screen. They started the study phase by a button press. Then the first study list of 30 words was presented item by item. The temporal sequence of its presentation was as follows (see Figure 2.1). After a fixation point (+) had been presented at the center of the screen for 200 ms the screen was erased. 400 ms later the study item was presented for 250 ms. The word was followed by a 2500 ms delay (blank screen). Thereafter either an M or a V was presented for 2500 ms. These letters were used as a cue to indicate whether the preceding word was a TBR (M - "merken", Engl. *remember*) or a TBF (V - "vergessen", Engl. *forget*) item. After another 900 ms the next trial started. To strengthen the differential instruction for TBR and TBF items in the study blocks each block was followed by a free recall test for TBR items: the words "bitte aufschreiben" (Engl. *please write down*) were presented for 60 s, while the participants wrote down as many TBR items as they could recall. A separate sheet of paper was used for each block. After one minute elapsed, a beep sounded, and after another 5 s the presentation of the next list started.

After all six lists had been presented, there was a 15 min retention interval in which the participants performed two attentional tests in order to reduce active rehearsal of the study items. Instructions for the recognition test were given immediately before the test phase. In the recognition test participants held a small response box on their lap. The 180 previously studied words and the 180 new words were presented in randomized order. The temporal sequence of item presentation was as follows. Trials began with the presentation of a fixation point for 200 ms. 400 ms later the test item was presented for 250 ms. Participants were instructed to judge whether or not the test item had been seen in the study phase, irrespective whether it was a TBR or TBF item, signaling their responses by immediately pressing one of two buttons. 2500 ms after the offset of item presentation the next trial started. There was a brief rest break after 180 test items. The button assignments were counterbalanced across participants such that there was no systematic influence of the hands used for old/new judgments.

- study phase

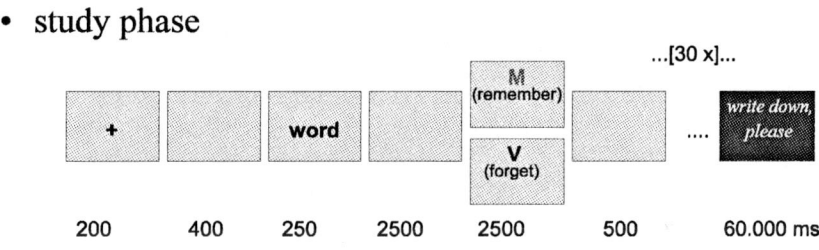

- recognition test

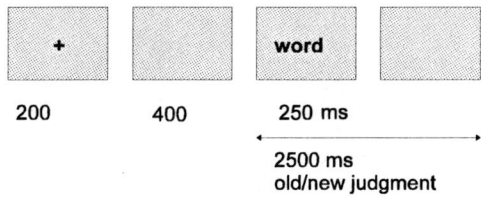

Figure 2.1 Time course of the study phase and recognition test in Experiment 1.

2.1.4 ERP recording

The EEG activity was recorded with Ag/AgCl electrodes mounted in an elastic cap (Electrocap International) from 61 scalp sites of the extended ten-twenty system. The spatial layout of the scalp electrodes is displayed in Fig. 2.2.

Electrode labeling is based on the standard nomenclature described in Sharbrough et al. (1990). The ground electrode was positioned 10% of the distance between the two preoccular points right to Cz. The vertical electrooculogram (EOG) was recorded from electrodes located above and below the right eye. The horizontal EOG was recorded from

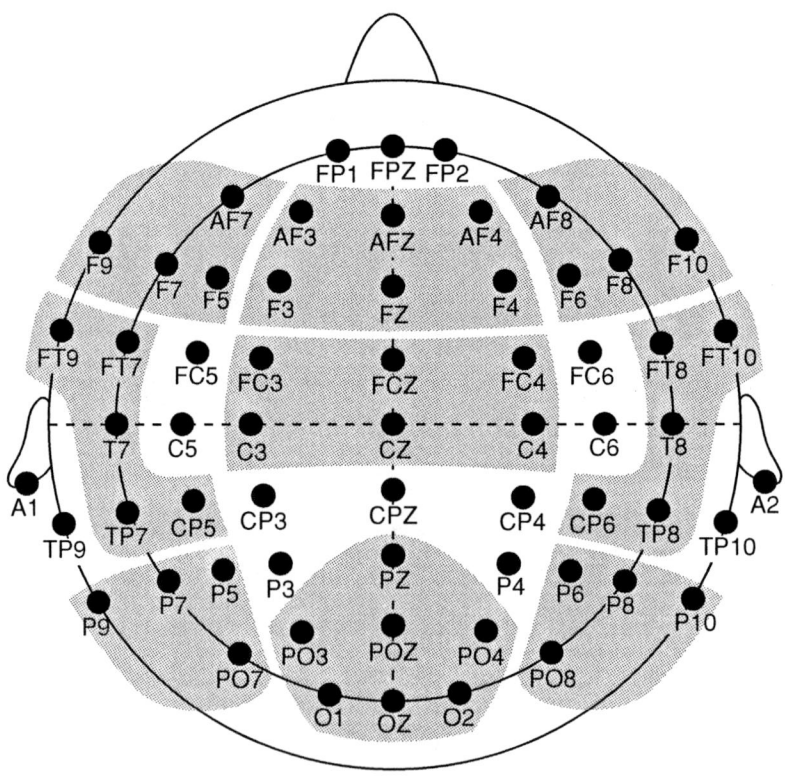

Figure 2.2 Layout of the locations of the 61 scalp electrodes used for ERP recording. The shaded areas mark the 9 regions of interest used for statistical analyses.

electrodes positioned at the outer canthus of each eye. Electrode impedance was kept below 5 kΩ. The right mastoid was recorded as an additional channel. All scalp electrodes were referenced to the left mastoid and were off-line rereferenced to linked mastoids. The EEG and EOG were recorded continuously with a band pass from DC to 30 Hz and were A-D converted with 16 bit resolution at a sampling rate of 250 Hz.

2.1.5 Data analysis

Behavioral data. Reaction time was defined as the interval between the appearance of the test items and the participants' keypress. The reaction times were averaged separately for each item type and response category.

ERP data. In the study phase separate ERPs were computed for each participant at all recording sites with epochs extending from 200 ms before word onset until 2000 ms thereafter and from 200 ms before the cue until 2000 ms thereafter. According to subsequent memory performance in the recognition test, they were selectively averaged for TBR items classified as old, TBF items classified as old, and TBF items classified as new. Because of too small number of artifact free trials for TBR items subsequently classified as new to form reliable ERPs, this category could not be investigated

In the test phase ERPs were computed for each participant at all recording sites with epochs extending from 200 ms before onset of word presentation until 1800 ms thereafter. They were selectively averaged for TBR items classified as old, TBF items classified as old, and new items classified as new (correct rejections). Because of too small numbers of artifact free trials for study items classified as new and new items classified as old (false alarms) to form reliable ERPs, those categories were not investigated. In order to examine ERP old/new effects for TBR and TBF items, difference waves between ERPs to recognized words and correct rejections were computed separately for both item types.

The average voltages in the 200 ms preceding the items were examined for systematic differences as a function of the experimental conditions described above. Because no systematic effects were found, this epoch served as a baseline, i.e., its mean value was subtracted from each data point in the waveforms. In a first step, the EEG epochs were scanned for muscular and large EOG artifacts. Whenever the standard deviation in a 200 ms interval exceeded 50 µV, the epoch was rejected. In a second step, remaining small horizontal and vertical EOG artifacts which were still present in the EEG signal were corrected by an eye movement correction procedure (Pfeifer, 1993) based on a linear regression method described by Gratton et al. (1983).

Because some of the ERP components were not clearly visible as peaks at all electrode sites, mean amplitude measures were considered more reliable for component scoring than peak measures (cf. Hoormann et al., 1998). The respective time intervals used for quantification of the ERP responses will be reported in the result section. In order to avoid the loss of statistical power that occurs when repeated-measure ANOVAs are used to quantify multi-channel and multi-time window data (Gevins et al., 1995, 1996; Oken & Chiappa, 1986), electrode sites were pooled to form nine topographical regions. Given that many cognitive ERP components are generated by multiple brain areas and widespread populations of neurons, the approach of collapsing measures across nearby recordings sites implicitly recognizes the limits of functional localization that can be expected with scalp-recorded ERPs. Moreover, it is conceivable that electrode placement varies with respect to cortical anatomy, because of individual differences in head size and shape as well as brain morphology. Statistical analyses of broad regions of interest serve to accommodate these individual differences. The following regions were defined: left frontal (F9, F7, F5, AF7); medial frontal (AF3, AFz, AF4, F3, Fz, F4); right frontal (F10, F8, F6, AF8); left temporal (FT9, FT7, T7, TP7, CP5); medial central (FC3, FCz, FC4, C3, Cz, C4); right temporal (FT10, FT8, T8, TP8, CP6); left parieto-occipital (P9, P7, P5, PO7); medial parieto-occipital (Pz, PO3, POz, PO4, O1, Oz, O2); and right parieto-occipital (P10, P8, P6, PO8). According to Homan *et al.* (1987), Lagerlund et al. (1993) and Towle et al. (1993), who established a correspondence between electrode site and underlying cerebral structure using radiographic or magnetic resonance imaging techniques, the medial frontal region is approximately over the middle frontal gyrus (Brodman area (BA) 46). The left and right frontal regions are approximately over the inferior frontal gyri (BA 45). The left and right temporal regions cover approximately the middle and superior temporal gyri (BA 21 and 22), whereas the medial central region is approximately over the precentral gyrus (BA 4). Finally, the left and right parieto-occipital regions cover approximately the posterior part of the middle temporal gyri and the anterior occipital sulcus, whereas the medial parieto-occipital region is approximately over the occipital gyri and the superior parietal lobe (BA 17, 7). The location of these nine regions on the scalp is indicated by the shaded areas in Figure 2.2. For statistical analysis a single mean amplitude was obtained for each area in each time window by averaging the mean amplitudes from the channels within the area, similarly as in previous studies (e.g., Curran et al., 1993; Mecklinger, 1998).

In the study phase ERPs time-locked to two events were analyzed separately: first, onset of word presentation, and second, onset of the cue. In both cases, three-way repeated-measure ANOVAs with the factors item/response type (3 levels), lateral dimension (3 levels), and anterior-posterior dimension (3 levels) were performed. Moreover, for the cue-locked data the latency and amplitudes of the P300 component at the Pz electrode were subjected to a one-way ANOVA with the factor item/response type (3 levels). In case of significant interactions involving the item/response type factor, one-way ANOVAs with the factor item/response type were performed to examine the effects of this factor in each of the topographical regions.

The ERP measures from the recognition test were analyzed in three steps. First, it was tested whether recognition of TBR and TBF items evoked reliable old/new effects by subjecting the ERP measures to a four-way repeated-measure ANOVA with factors anterior-posterior dimension (a-p dimension) (3 levels), lateral dimension (3 levels), time window (3 levels) and item/response type (3 levels, i.e., recognized TBR, recognized TBF, correct rejections). In a second step, three-way repeated-measure ANOVAs with factors anterior-posterior dimension (a-p dimension) (3 levels), lateral dimension (3 levels) and item type (2 levels) were conducted on the ERP difference measures (recognized TBR minus correct rejections, recognized TBF minus correct rejections) separately for the three time windows. In case of significant interactions involving the item/response type factor, one-way ANOVAs with the factor item/response type were performed to examine the effects of this factor in each of the topographical regions. When interactions were accompanied by main effects of item/response type, measures of treatment magnitude (Ω^2; cf. Keppel, 1991)[6] for the single effects of item type will also be reported. All effects with more than one degree of freedom in

---

[6] Ω^2 is a relative measure of treatment magnitude or effect strength, reflecting the proportional amount of the total variance that can be attributed to the variations among the experimental treatments. The index can range from 0 to 1, and, according to Cohen (1977), an effect is considered *large* if it produces an Ω^2 of 0.15 or greater.

the numerator were adjusted for violations of sphericity according to the formula of Greenhouse and Geisser (1959). In order to avoid reporting large amounts of statistical results not relevant for the issues under investigation, only main effects or interactions including the item/response type factor will be reported. Scalp potential topographic maps were generated using a two-dimensional spherical spline interpolation (Perrin et al., 1989) and a radial projection from Cz, which respects the length of the median arcs.

Topographic profile comparisons

For the present study it was of high importance whether the old/new effects elicited by TBR and TBF words differed topographically or not. Only a topographical difference indicates that different neuronal activities could be involved in retrieval of the two item types. As noted by McCarthy & Wood (1985), ANOVA is based on an additive model, whereas ERP components are multiplicative in nature. For example, a doubling of strength of a component generator leads to a doubling of amplitudes at each electrode. This results not only in a main effect, but usually also in an interaction, because the additive enhancement of the component is larger at the peak than at the flanks. In such cases, it would be misleading to interpret the significant interaction as a difference in topography, because the real reason for this difference is obviously an enhancement in generator strength. Therefore, data of each condition have to be rescaled such that amplitude differences between the two contrasted conditions are removed (McCarthy & Wood, 1985). In the present study this was achieved by z-score normalization of the data for each analyzed electrode. If an interaction of condition and topographical location factors is found after rescaling, this can be interpreted as a topographical difference between the two contrasted conditions. Therefore in a third step, the same three-way repeated-measure ANOVAs as mentioned above were conducted on the rescaled old/new difference measures, in order to test whether the old/new effects differ topographically.

2.2 Experiment 2 - ERP study of depth of encoding

2.2.1 Participants

Twenty volunteers (12 female) between 19 and 29 years of age (mean: 23.2 years) participated in this experiment. All participants were students at the University of Leipzig. They reported to be in good health and had normal or corrected-to-normal vision and gave written informed consent prior to the experiment. For their participation they were paid 13 DM per hour. The participants of the two experiments were matched for age, gender and socioeconomic status[7].

2.2.2 Stimuli and procedure

In Experiment 2 the same single word cueing method and the same stimulus material were used as in Experiment 1. The time course of the experiment is depicted in Figure 3. In the study phase memory encoding was manipulated by cueing participants to process the presented word either deeply or shallowly. The presentation of each word was followed by either an S (S - 'Satz', Engl. *sentence*) or a B (B - 'Buchstabe', Engl. *letter*). By means of the 'S' cue participants were requested to form a sentence containing the presented word as a subject. After the 'B' cue they had to decide whether the letter E is contained in the presented word, thus the respective item was encoded shallowly. The oral responses in both encoding tasks were recorded on DAT-tapes. After the presentation of all 30 items of a study block participants were requested to count aloud backwards for 60 seconds, beginning from a presented random number and decrementing stepwise by three. As in Experiment 1, six study blocks, i.e., a total of 180 words, were presented. The retention delay and the recognition test were identical to Experiment 1.

---

[7] It was not possible to perform both experiments with the same participants because the verbal stimulus material was limited to 360 words. The experiments were performed with a distance of only a few weeks, such that the results of Experiment 2 could have been confounded, if the participants had already studied the same items in the directed forgetting paradigm.

- study phase

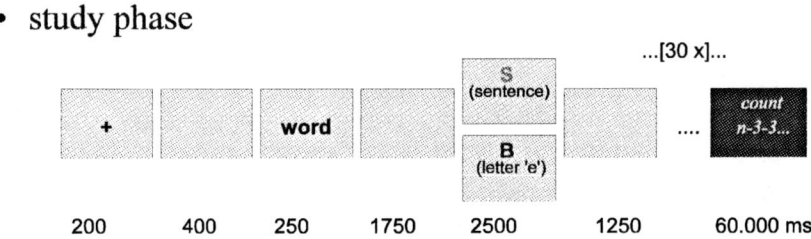

- recognition test

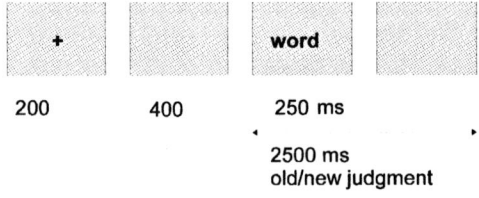

Figure 2.3 Time course of the study phase and the recognition test in Experiment 2.

2.2.3 ERP recording and data analysis

The procedure for EEG recording and data analysis were performed as in Experiment 1 with the following exceptions: The EEG activity was recorded with Electrocap tin electrodes. Because of a high amount of movement-related activity due to articulation, the ERPs recorded in the study phase could not be investigated. In the test phase ERPs were selectively averaged for correct responses to deeply encoded items, shallowly encoded items classified as old, and new items. Because of too small numbers of artifact free trials to form reliable ERPs for study items classified as new (misses) and new items classified as old (false alarms), those categories were not investigated. In addition, difference waves of ERPs to recognized words

40

and correct rejections were computed for deeply and shallowly encoded items, respectively. Artifact rejection was performed as described in Experiment 1. In addition, EEG data of 4 participants were highpass filtered with 0.15 Hz to remove the influence of DC drifts. Statistical analysis of the ERP data was performed as in Experiment 1, except that different time windows were used for the quantification of ERP effects.

Chapter 3

Hypotheses

From the paradigm employed in Experiment 1 it follows that differential encoding for TBR and TBF was involved up to a certain extent. The immediate recall test for TBR words after presentation of each block of 30 items presumably lead to rehearsal of the TBR words via retrieval practice. The inclusion of an immediate recall test after each study block aimed at familiarizing the subjects with the forget instruction. However, the drawback of this procedure is that it was not possible to test the differential encoding model directly against the retrieval inhibition model. Rather the main question of the present study was: is there *differential encoding alone* or *differential encoding plus retrieval inhibition*? The following hypotheses are based on the to-be-tested current opinion that in a single-item-cueing procedure of directed forgetting differential encoding (i.e., selective rehearsal and elaborative processing of TBR items) *alone* is responsible for the directed forgetting effect (e.g., Basden et al., 1993; Basden & Basden, 1998; Wilson & Kipp, 1998).

3.1 Study phase - encoding

In Experiment 1, ERPs recorded during the study phase were examined. It was examined,

(1) whether in the word-cue interval subsequent memory effects for both item types can be found, which would indicate that the items were encoded before the cue appeared,

(2) whether the functional relevance of the cue (remember vs. forget) has an ERP correlate,

(3) whether subsequent memory effects after cue presentation can be distinguished based on memory performance in the recognition test. A difference in post-cue SMEs between TBR and TBF words would be a direct indication that TBF material is encoded in a different way than TBR items. This difference could be present in amplitude and/or in scalp topography. As noted in Section 1.3.2.1, the amplitude of the SME is influenced by the amount of semantic (deep) processing. Thus, according to the differential encoding model the SME for TBR words should be larger than for TBF words. In addition, there could be topographical differences: a positive, late frontal slow potential as a correlate of elaborative processing could be expected for TBR items (Donchin & Fabiani, 1991; Mecklinger & Müller, 1996). Given that TBF items are not processed elaboratively, no such late frontal SME should be found for those words.

3.2 Recognition test - retrieval

3.2.1 Experiment 1

The goal of the recognition test in the first experiment was to examine whether ERP old/new effects elicited by recognition of TBR and TBF items differ in their temporal or spatial character. According to current knowledge about the electrophysiological correlates of recognition memory (cf. Section 1.3.2.2), predictions can be made with respect to the differential encoding model of directed forgetting (cf. Section 1.2.2.2). First, if the early frontal old/new effect is associated with a feeling of familiarity for previously studied items it should not differ for TBF and TBR items because both presumably are similarly encoded before participants are cued to either remember or forget the word. This view that familiarity should be the same for both item types is supported by the findings of Gardiner et al. (1994), who employed a Remember/Know procedure in a directed forgetting paradigm and found only for consciously recollected items a directed forgetting effect, while the amount of familiarity based recognition judgments did not differ between TBR and TBF. Second, if solely differential encoding is responsible for the lower recognition performance of TBF items, memory traces of TBR items would be of considerably higher strength than those of TBF items. Thus the parietal old/new effect would be expected to be smaller in magnitude for TBF items than for TBR items. Under the assumption that the late right frontal old/new effect reflects processes that act on the products of retrieval and that include the reconstruction of information from the study episode, the amplitude of this effect should be reduced for TBF items, because fewer study phase information is available.

3.2.2 Experiment 2

In order to prove whether the ERP patterns obtained in the directed forgetting paradigm can be explained by the differential encoding model, a *second experiment* was conducted to examine the influence of differential encoding on recognition-related ERP old/new effects directly. To guarantee maximal compatibility of both experiments the same stimulus materials and single-item-cueing method as in Experiment 1 were employed. Upon presentation of the cue, participants had to either deeply or shallowly encode the foregoing item. Presuming that the differences in memory performance in Experiment 1 were due to differential encoding, i. e. shallow processing of TBF items and deep processing of TBR items, the spatio-temporal patterns of old/new effects should be similar in both experiments. Alternatively, if directed forgetting effects do not result from differential encoding alone, then the ERP pattern evoked by deeply and shallowly encoded test items should be qualitatively different from those obtained in Experiment 1.

More specifically, based on the current knowledge about recognition-related ERPs, one can predict that: first, the early frontal old/new effect should not differ between deeply and shallowly encoded items, because familiarity should be the same for both item types (Gardiner, 1988); second, the weaker memory trace of the shallowly encoded words should result in a reduced parietal old/new effect; and third, for shallowly encoded words the late right frontal old/new effect should be of smaller magnitude, given that less contextual information is retrieved for those items.

Summary

Under the assumption that in both experiments the mechanism separating remembering from forgetting and deep from shallow processing is differential encoding, the hypotheses about the ERP patterns can be summarized as shown in the following table:

Table 3.1 Expected patterns of old/new effects in both experiments under the assumption that solely differential encoding is involved.(+/++: large/very large old/new effect).

	directed forgetting		depth of processing	
	to-be-remembered	to-be-forgotten	deeply encoded	shallowly encoded
early frontal effect	+ ═	+	+ ═	+
parietal effect	++ >	+	++ >	+
late right frontal effect	++ >	+	++ >	+

Chapter 4

Results

4.1 Experiment 1

4.1.1 Behavioral data

Mean reaction times and recognition rates for TBR and TBF words, correct rejections and false alarms are displayed in Table 4.1 and in Figure 4.1. Participants responded faster to TBR than to TBF and new items and the recognition rate for TBR words was 30.1 percent higher than for TBF words. Thus, the directed forgetting procedure was successful. This pattern of results was confirmed by statistical analyses. Repeated-measure ANOVA with the factor item/response type revealed a main effect for reaction times ($F(2, 38) = 70.92$, $p < 0.0001$) and for recognition rates ($F(2, 38) = 473.20$, $p < 0.0001$). Additional analyses

Table 4.1 Mean reaction times, proportion of correct responses and false alarm rates in Experiment 1.

	correct responses			false alarms
	TBR	TBF	new	
reaction time (ms)	695 (17.3)	820 (30.1)	862 (26.4)	898 (34.1)
percent of presented items	89.1 (1.5)	59.0 (2.0)	82.8 (2.3)	16.6 (2.1)

Standard error of the mean in parentheses.

47

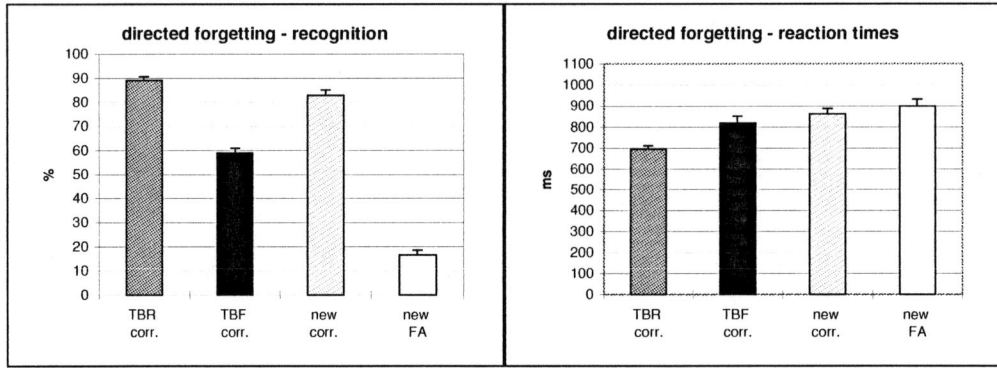

Figure 4.1 Behavioral results obtained in Experiment 1: Recognition rates and false alarm rate in percent of presented items (left side), reaction times (right side); TBR = to-be-remembered items, TBF = to-be-forgotten items, new = new items, corr = correctly recognized, FA = false alarms.

contrasting correct responses to TBR and TBF items revealed a main effect of item type for reaction time ($F(1, 19) = 58.91$, $p < 0.0001$) and for recognition rates ($F(1, 19) = 145.35$, $p < 0.0001$).

4.1.2 ERP data

4.1.2.1 Study phase

Pre-cue ERPs

In the study phase ERPs time-locked to word presentation and to the cue were recorded. In Figure 4.2 the waveforms at three midline electrodes and at frontal, central and parietal recording sites elicited by presentation of TBR and TBF words and averaged separately according to subsequent recognition performance are depicted. Unfortunately, there were too few artifact free trials to form ERPs for subsequently not recognized TBR words. As can be seen in the figure, there are no significant differences between the waveforms for subsequently recognized TBR and TBF words. However, beginning at about 300 ms after word onset the ERP waveform elicited by subsequently recognized TBF items is more positive going than the ERP for not recognized TBF items. This subsequent memory effect (SME) is most pronounced at centroparietal electrodes and slightly shifted to the left

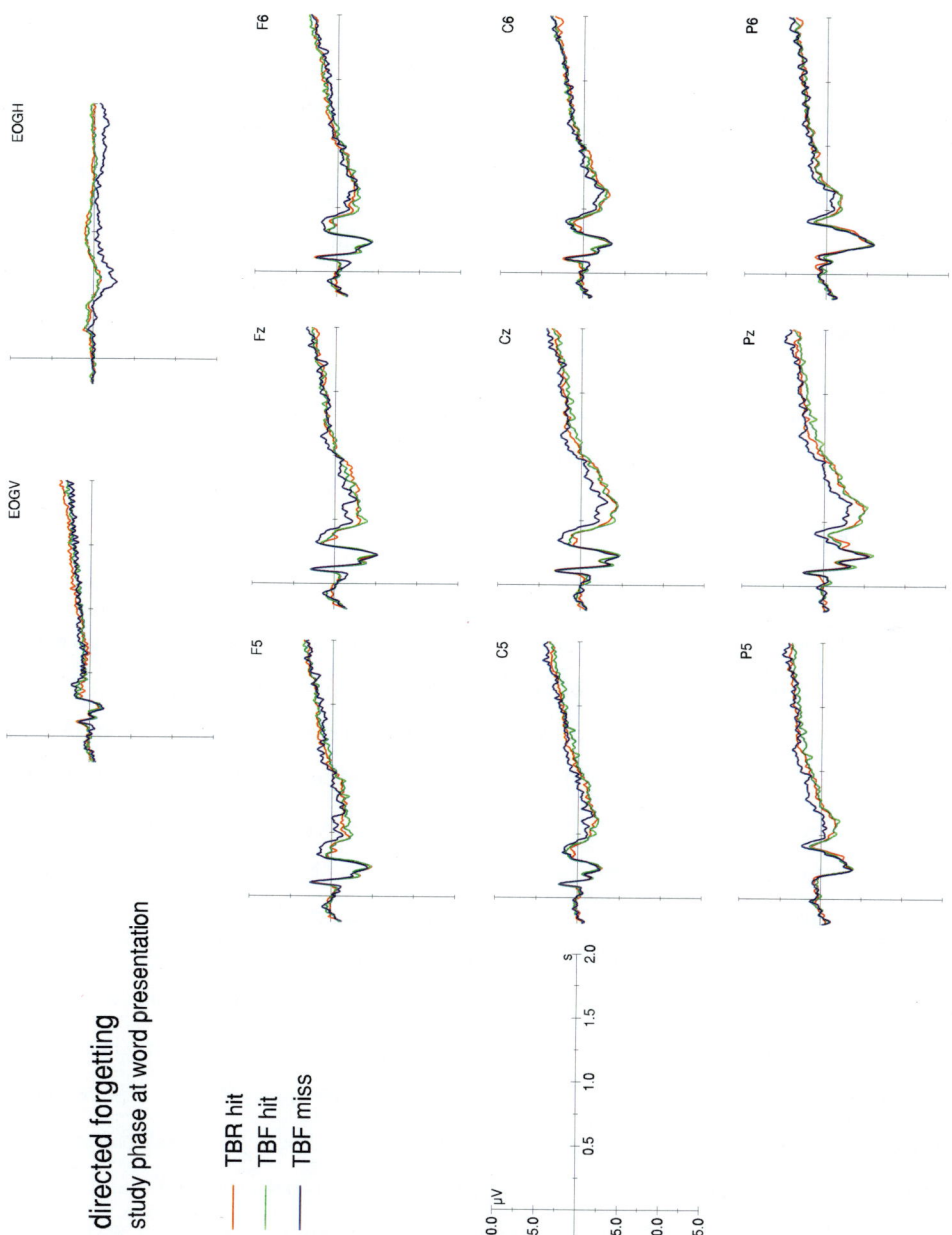

Figure 4.2 ERP waveforms elicited by recognized TBR and TBF items (hits) and by not recognized TBR words (misses) and averaged across subjects in the study phase at word presentation. In this and the following figures the waveforms are plotted for nine electrodes representing the left, medial and right frontal (F5, Fz, F6), central (C5, Cz, C6), and parietal (P5, Pz, P6) regions. The vertical lines indicate the onset of word presentation. EOGV: vertical electrooculogram, EOGH: horizontal electrooculogram.

49

Table 4.2 ANOVA results for ERP measures in the study phase at word presentation.

	df	F-values
I/R type	2, 38	3.45†
I/R type × lat dim	4, 76	3.00*
I/R type × a-p dim	4, 76	0.19
I/R type × a-p dim × lat dim	8, 152	0.96

Note: I/R type = item/response type (recognized TBR and TBF items, and correct rejections); time = time window; lat dim = lateral dimension; a-p dim = anterior-posterior dimension; † = $p < 0.10$; * = $p < 0.05$; ** = $p < 0.01$.

hemisphere. The difference of the waveforms lasts for about 1000 ms. These observations were proved by statistical analysis performed for a time window lasting from 300 to 750 ms after word onset. The results of a three-way ANOVA with the factors item-response type (3 levels), lateral dimension (3 levels), and anterior-posterior dimension (3 levels) are displayed in Table 4.2. Based on the interaction item/response type × lateral dimension and the marginally significant main effect of item/response type separate ANOVAs contrasting item/response types were performed. The ANOVA contrasting the ERP data elicited by subsequently recognized TBR and TBF items did not give rise to any significant main effect or interaction ($ps > 0.57$) indicating that there is no significant difference between the two waveforms. In the comparison of recognized and unrecognized TBF items the main effect of response type (F (1, 19) = 4.58; $p < 0.05$) and the interaction item/response type × lateral dimension (F (2, 38) = 3.78; $p < 0.05$) were significant. Post hoc tests revealed significant main effects of item/response type only for the left (F (1, 19) = 6.46; $p < 0.05$) and midline regions (F (1, 19) = 5.38; $p < 0.05$) indicating that the subsequent memory effect was slightly lateralized to the left.

Post-cue ERPs

The ERP waveforms for the same three item-response types at cue presentation are shown in Figure 4.3. A strong effect of cue on the P300 component is most striking. For subsequently recognized items the P300 elicited by the remember cue has a shorter latency and higher amplitude than the P300 evoked by the forget cue. The peak values of the P300 for the three item/response types are displayed in Table 4.3.

Table 4.3 Mean peak values of the P300 component at Pz in the study phase at cue presentation

Item/response type	Latency (ms)	Amplitude (µV)
TBR hit	353 (8.7)	20.0 (1.27)
TBF hit	401 (13.3)	15.4 (1.25)
TBF miss	418 (14.2)	13.0 (1.54)

ANOVA with the factors item/response type (3 levels) and P300 peak latency was performed. For the latency measures a main effect of item/response type was revealed (F (2, 38) = 19.36, $p < 0.0001$). The planned comparison contrasting recognized TBR and TBF items also revealed a significant main effect of item type (F (1, 19) = 16.55; $p < 0.001$). The contrast between the P300 latencies of recognized and unrecognized TBF items gave rise to a main effect of response type (F (1, 19) = 6.37; $p < 0.05$). These results indicate, that both the type of cue and subsequent response have influence on the latency of the P300 component.

Comparing the waveforms for subsequently recognized and non-recognized TBF items, also at time of cue presentation an additional difference is visible subsequent to the P300: the later recognized TBF words elicited a more positive going waveform, with this difference lasting from 250 ms until about 600 ms and being most pronounced at parietal electrodes. For statistical analysis a time window lasting from 300 to 600 ms after cue onset was chosen. The results of the three-way ANOVA with the factors item-response type

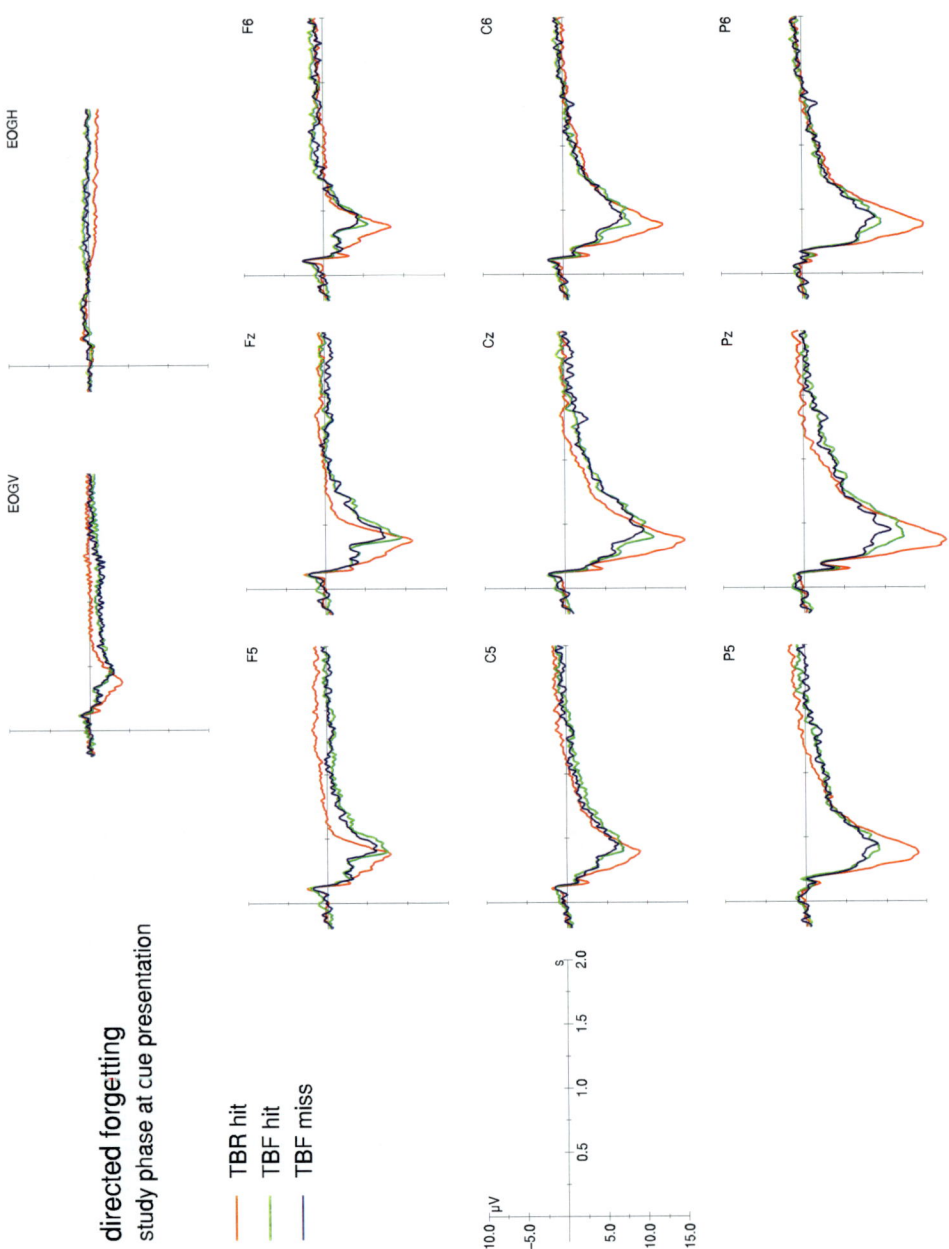

Figure 4.3 ERP waveforms elicited by recognized TBR and TBF items (hits) and by not recognized TBR words (misses) and averaged across subjects in the study phase at cue presentation. The vertical lines indicate the onset of cue presentation.

52

(3 levels), lateral dimension (3 levels), and anterior-posterior dimension (3 levels) are displayed in Table 4.4. Based on the significant interactions separate ANOVAs were performed to compare the ERP waveforms for TBR and TBF words and to recognized and unrecognized words. The ANOVA contrasting subsequently recognized TBR and TBF items revealed a significant main effect of item type (F (1, 19) = 13.24; $p < 0.0017$) and the interactions item type $\times$ lateral dimension (F (2, 38) = 3.83; $p < 0.0345$), item type $\times$ anterior-posterior dimension (F (2, 38) = 26.90; $p < 0.0001$), and item type $\times$ lateral dimension $\times$ anterior-posterior dimension (F (4, 76) = 7.56; $p < 0.001$). These interactions indicate that the

Table 4.4 ANOVA results for ERP measures in the study phase at cue presentation

	df	F-values
I/R type	2, 38	12.29‡
I/R type $\times$ lat dim	4, 76	3.54*
I/R type $\times$ a-p dim	4, 76	22.08‡
I/R type $\times$ a-p dim $\times$ lat dim	8, 152	4.00**

I/R type = item/response type (recognized TBR and TBF items, and correct rejections); time = time window; lat dim = lateral dimension; a-p dim = anterior-posterior dimension;
* = $p < 0.05$; ** = $p < 0.01$; † = $p < 0.005$; ‡ = $p < 0.0005$.

difference in P300 amplitude was - according to the typical distribution of this component - most pronounced at central and posterior recording sites (main effects of item type at central (F (1, 19) = 10.19; $p < 0.0048$) and posterior areas (F (1, 19) = 48.49; $p < 0.0001$)).

The ANOVA contrasting recognized and unrecognized TBF items revealed a significant interaction response type $\times$ lateral dimension $\times$ anterior-posterior dimension (F (4, 76) = 4.54; $p < 0.0072$). This was due to the fact that the difference between the two waveforms was significant only at posterior midline and right recording sites, as revealed by main effects of response type (midline area: F (1, 19) = 4.44, $p < 0.0486$; right area: F (1, 19) = 5.64, $p < 0.0282$).

4.1.2.2 Recognition test

Old/new effects for TBR and TBF items

Figure 4.4 displays the ERP waveforms at three midline electrodes and at lateral frontal, central and parietal recording sites elicited by old and new items in the recognition test. Starting around 300 ms the waveforms evoked by old items were more positive going than for new items. These old/new effects were observable for both TBR and TBF hits but differed in amplitude and topographical distribution. Recognition of TBR words elicited three temporally and topographically distinct old/new effects. An early phasic, frontal positivity with a maximum at midline electrodes could be observed in a time window 300-550 ms. Starting around 400 ms and extending until around 900 ms a parietally distributed phasic positive wave, slightly lateralized to the left overlapped the early frontal old/new effect. Finally, a sustained positive slow wave was observable over right frontal recording sites. This late right frontal old/new effect started at about 700 ms and extended until 1600 ms post stimulus onset.

For recognized TBF items only the early frontomedial and the late right frontal positive old/new effects occurred, whereas the parietal old/new effect was virtually absent for TBF items. The early frontomedial positivity is less pronounced for TBF items than for TBR items. Interestingly, the amplitude of the late right frontal positive slow wave was larger for TBF hits than for TBR hits.

In order to capture the three hypothesized components of the old/new effect that were apparent in the waveforms, three time windows were selected for statistical analysis: an early (350 550 ms), a middle (550-850 ms), and a late (950-1200 ms) time window. The results of the omnibus four-way ANOVA which was performed in order to test whether both item types elicited old/new effects are displayed in Table 4.5.

Based on the interactions time window × item type × lateral dimension × anterior-posterior dimension three-way ANOVAs with the factors response type (2 levels), lateral and anterior-posterior dimensions were performed separately for each time window. These ANOVAs contrasted hits and correct rejections separately for TBR and TBF items.

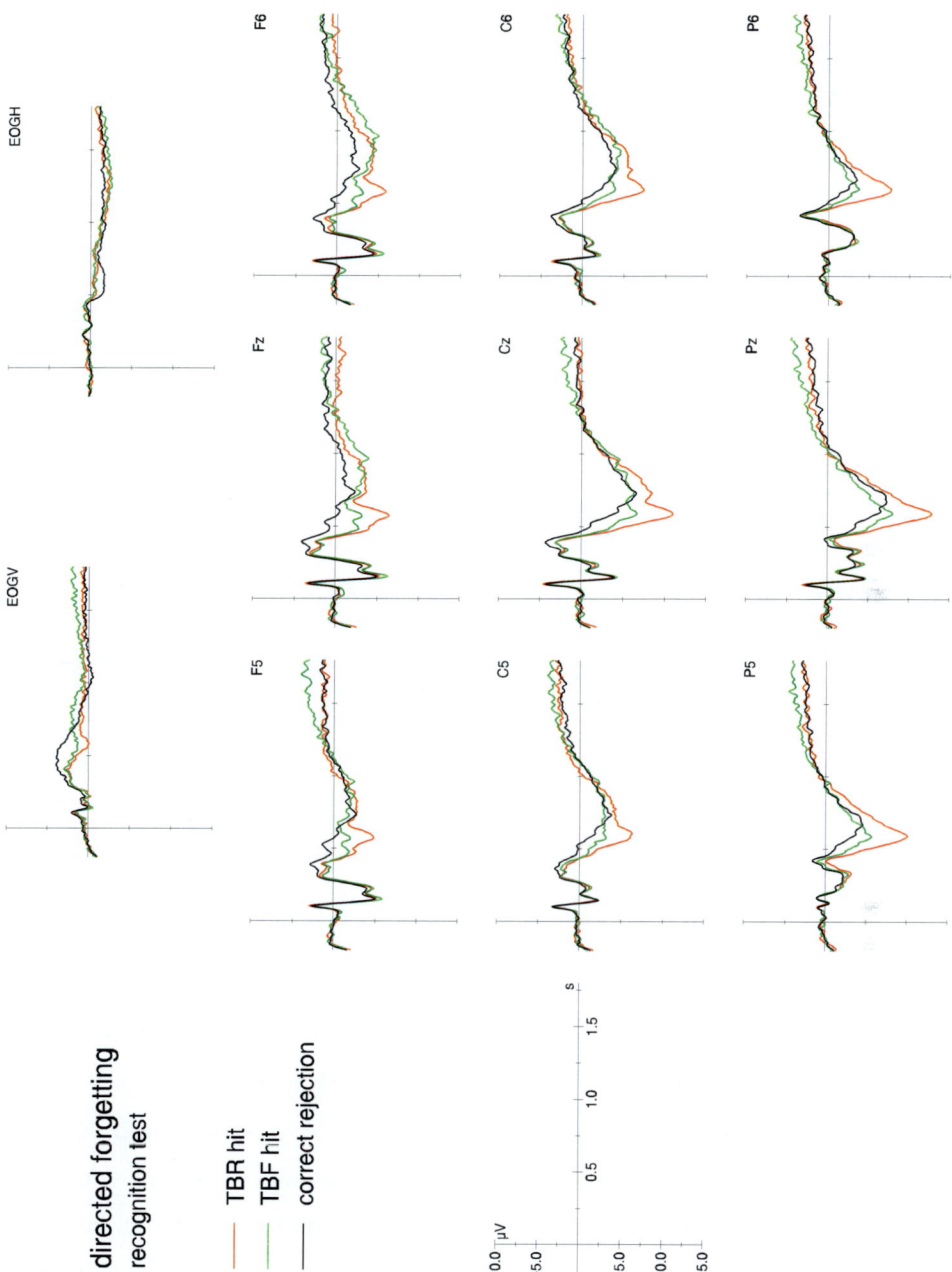

Figure 4.4 ERP waveforms elicited by recognized TBR and TBF items and by correctly rejected new items and averaged across subjects at recognition test.

Table 4.5 Experiment 1: ANOVA results for ERP measures in the recognition test

	df	F-values
I/R type	2, 38	8.94**
I/R type × time	4, 76	14.58‡
I/R type × time × lat dim	8, 152	4.98†
I/R type × time × a-p dim	8, 152	2.18
I/R type × time × a-p dim × lat dim	16, 304	2.77*
I/R type × lat dim	4, 76	4.79†
I/R type × a-p dim	4, 76	5.92*
I/R type × a-p dim × lat dim	8, 152	5.83†

I/R type = item/response type (recognized TBR and TBF items, and correct rejections); time = time window;
lat dim = lateral dimension; a-p dim = anterior-posterior dimension;
* = $p < 0.05$; ** = $p < 0.01$; † = $p < 0.005$; ‡ = $p < 0.0005$.

In the early time interval for TBR items a significant main effect of response type ($F(1,$ 19) = 76.68, $p < 0.0001$), the interaction of response type × lateral dimension ($F(2, 38)$ = 20.97, $p < 0.0001$), and the triple interaction response type × lateral dimension × anterior-posterior dimension ($F(4, 76) = 9.82, p < 0.0001$) were obtained. In the same time interval the ANOVA for TBF items revealed a main effect of response type ($F(1, 19) = 20.45, p < 0.001$), and the interactions of response type × lateral dimension ($F(2, 38) = 10.61, p < 0.001$), response type × anterior-posterior dimension ($F(2, 38) = 5.60, p < 0.05$), and the triple interaction response type × lateral dimension × anterior-posterior dimension ($F(4, 76) = 6.80, p < 0.001$) were significant. One-way ANOVAs indicated that in the early time window for both item types the old/new differences were significant at all regions ($ps < 0.05$), except for TBF items at the right posterior region ($p = 0.058$). The highest treatment magnitudes were obtained for the frontal and central midline recordings (TBR: $\Omega^2 = 0.79$ and 0.78, TBF: $\Omega^2 =$ 0.56 and 0.53). Moreover, for TBR items the treatment magnitude showed a maximum at the left posterior region ($\Omega^2 = 0.80$), suggesting that the parietal old/new effect has its onset already in the early time window.

ANOVAs contrasting the ERP data elicited by correctly recognized TBR items and by correct rejections in the middle time window gave rise to a significant main effect of response type ($F(1, 19) = 28.28, p < 0.0001$), the interaction response type $\times$ lateral dimension ($F(2, 38)$ = 5.49, $p < 0.05$), and the triple interaction response type $\times$ lateral dimension $\times$ anterior-posterior dimension ($F(4, 76) = 5.34, p < 0.05$). An ANOVA for frontal regions revealed a slight lateralization to the right (main effect of response type ($F(1, 19) = 14.85, p < 0.005$), interaction response type $\times$ lateral dimension ($F(2, 38) = 6.52, p < 0.05$), indicating an overlap with the onset of the late right frontal positivity. This was confirmed by separate one-way tests revealing significant main effects of response type for all regions ($ps < 0.05$). The treatment magnitudes amounted to Ω^2 = 0.21, 0.53, and 0.43 for the left, middle and right frontal regions, respectively. The ANOVA for central regions revealed a main effect of response type ($F(1, 19) = 25.37, p < 0.0001$), an interaction response type $\times$ lateral dimension ($F(2, 38)$ = 9.44, $p < 0.005$) reflecting a slight lateralization to the left. One-way ANOVAs revealed significant old/new effects at all regions ($ps < 0.05$), however, the highest treatment magnitude was obtained for the midline site ($\Omega^2 = 0.61$).

For TBF items in the middle time interval only a triple interaction response type $\times$ lateral dimension $\times$ anterior-posterior dimension ($F(4, 76) = 3.43, p < 0.05$) could be observed. One-way ANOVAs failed to reveal main effects of response type in any of the topographical regions ($ps > 0.14$).

In the late time window for TBR items the interactions response type $\times$ lateral dimension ($F(2, 38) = 6.39, p < 0.01$) and response type $\times$ lateral dimension $\times$ anterior-posterior dimension ($F(4, 76) = 3.16, p < 0.05$) were significant. The same analysis for TBF items revealed the interactions response type $\times$ lateral dimension ($F(2, 38) = 7.12, p < 0.005$) and response type $\times$ anterior-posterior dimension ($F(2, 38) = 16.45, p < 0.0005$), and the triple interaction response type $\times$ lateral dimension $\times$ anterior-posterior dimension ($F(4, 76) = 8.02, p < 0.0005$) to be significant. Planned comparisons indicated that the old/new differences were significant at the right frontal region ($p < 0.05$) with an effect size of $\Omega^2 = 0.20$ for TBR items and at right and medial frontal regions ($p < 0.05$), for TBF items with effect sizes of $\Omega^2 = 0.43$ and 0.34.

Between-condition comparison

   The foregoing analysis revealed differential old/new effects for TBR and TBF items in each of the three time windows. In a next step the old/new effects for both item types were compared directly using an ANOVA for the difference wave data (correctly recognized TBR items minus new; correctly recognized TBF items minus new). The results of the three-way ANOVAs for the three time windows are displayed in Table 4.6. The old/new effects for both item types at the three frontal and parietal topographical regions are illustrated in Fig. 4.5, and the corresponding scalp topographies are displayed in Fig. 4.6.

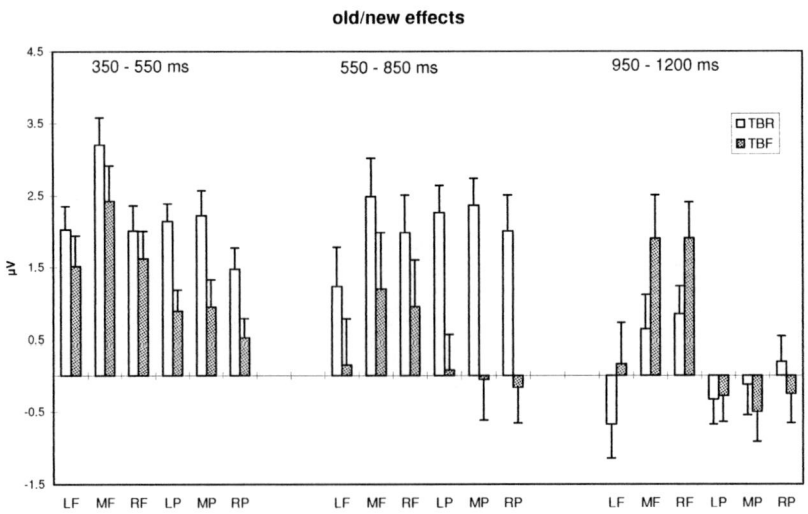

Figure 4.5 Mean difference between the amplitudes of the ERPs elicited by recognized and new items in the 350-550, 550-850, and 900-1300 ms latency regions, shown separately for to-be-remembered (TBR) and to-be-forgotten (TBF) items at frontal (LF, MF, RF) and posterior (LP, MP, RP) recording sites.

Table 4.6 ERP difference measures in Exp. 1: ANOVA results for the three time intervals in the recognition test

		F-values		
	df	350-550 ms	550-850 ms	950-1200 ms
Item type	1, 19	5.71*	12.14**	1.04
Item type × lat dim	2, 38	2.85	1.27	0.53
Item type × a-p dim	2, 38	2.66	4.88*	7.79**
Item type × lat dim × a-p dim	4, 76	0.70	1.66	2.96*

lat dim = lateral dimension; a-p dim = anterior-posterior dimension; * = $p < 0.05$; ** = $p < 0.01$.

In the early time interval a main effect of item type was obtained, reflecting the fact that old/new effects were larger for TBR than TBF items. No interactions with anterior-posterior or lateral dimension were found. These results and the topographical map for the early time window (Fig. 4.6) suggest that there were no topographical differences between the early frontal old/new effects elicited by TBR and TBF items. The ANOVA of the middle time window data revealed a main effect of item type and an interaction item type × anterior-posterior dimension. Inspection of the topographical map (Fig 4.6) and the magnitude of the old/new effects (Fig. 4.5) suggests that there were topographical differences between the two contrasted conditions due to the absence of the parietal subcomponent of the old/new effect for TBF item. This impression was confirmed by conducting the same ANOVA on the difference waves after they had been rescaled such that amplitude differences between the two contrasted conditions were removed (McCarthy & Wood, 1985), gave rise to the interaction item type × anterior-posterior dimension ($F(2, 38) = 4.58$, $p < 0.05$). This effect suggests that the old/new effects for TBR and TBF items in this interval arose from different combinations of neuronal sources (R. Johnson, 1993).

From the scalp topographies as depicted in Fig. 4.6 it is apparent that both TBR and TBF items elicited a late old/new effect with a maximum at right frontal recording sites.

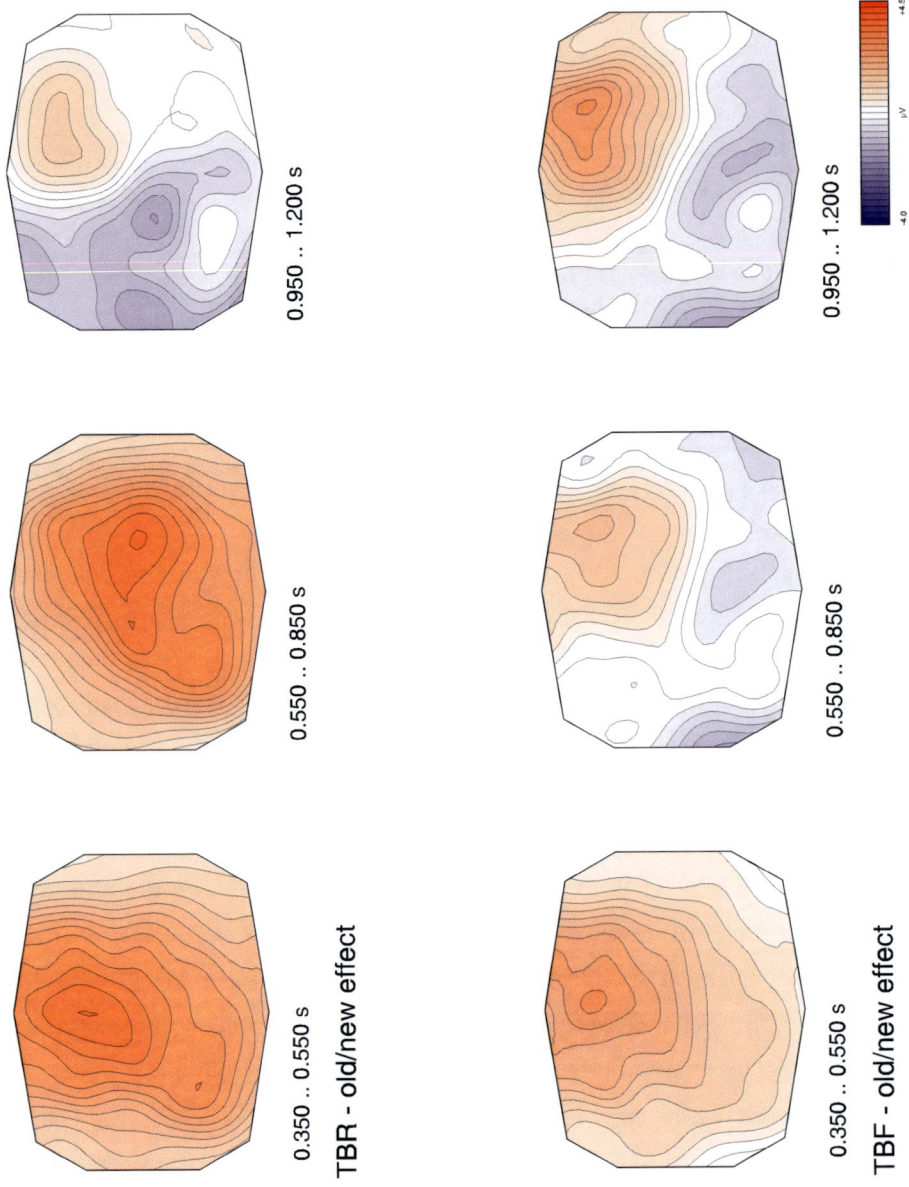

Figure 4.6 Topographic maps of the differences between ERPs for recognized and new items (old/new effects) in three time intervals. Upper row: to-be-remembered, lower row: to-be-forgotten words.

In the ANOVA of the data from the late time interval the interactions item type × anterior-posterior dimension and item type × lateral dimension × anterior-posterior dimension were significant, indicating that the magnitude of the old/new effects were larger for TBF than for TBR items at the right frontal region ($p < 0.05$, $\Omega^2 = 0.20$). At medial frontal regions the same difference of the old/new effects reached only marginal significance ($p = 0.055$). The ANOVA performed for the amplitude-normalized old/new differences revealed no significant interactions ($p > 0.18$), suggesting that the topographical distributions of the old/new effects for TBR and TBF items were statistically not different in the late time window.

In sum, the foregoing analyses revealed, that recognition of TBR items evoked three temporally and topographically distinct old/new effects, whereas TBF words elicited only two of these effects, namely an early frontomedial and a late right frontal positive old/new difference. No parietal old/new effect was found for TBF items. Moreover, the results revealed that the early frontomedial old/new effect was more pronounced for TBR items, whereas the late right frontal effect had a higher magnitude for TBF items.

4.2 Experiment 2

4.2.1 Behavioral data

Mean reaction time and recognition rates for deeply and shallowly encoded words, correct rejections and false alarms are displayed in Table 4.7 and in Figure 4.7. Response times were faster for deeply encoded items than for shallowly encoded and new items, and the difference in hit rates between the two item types amounted to 16.1 percent. This pattern of results was confirmed by statistical analyses. Repeated-measures ANOVA of correct responses with the factor item type revealed main effects for reaction times ($F(2, 38) = 24.20$, $p < 0.0001$) and for recognition rates ($F(2, 38) = 397.18$, $p < 0.0001$). Additional analyses contrasting deeply and shallowly encoded items revealed a main effect of encoding condition for reaction times ($F(1, 19) = 10.08$, $p < 0.01$) and for recognition rates ($F(1, 19) = 38.69$, $p < 0.0001$). In showing that deeply encoded words were classified faster and also more accurately than shallowly encoded words, the results demonstrate that our deep/shallow encoding instruction was successful.

Table 4.7 Mean reaction times, proportion of correct responses and false alarm rates in Experiment 2.

	correct responses			false alarms
	deeply encoded	shallowly encoded	new	
reaction time (ms)	806 (26.0)	865 (40.6)	947 (44.6)	1027 (56.1)
percent of presented items	89.7 (1.2)	73.3 (3.0)	82.3 (1.6)	17.1 (1.4)

Standard errors of the mean in parentheses.

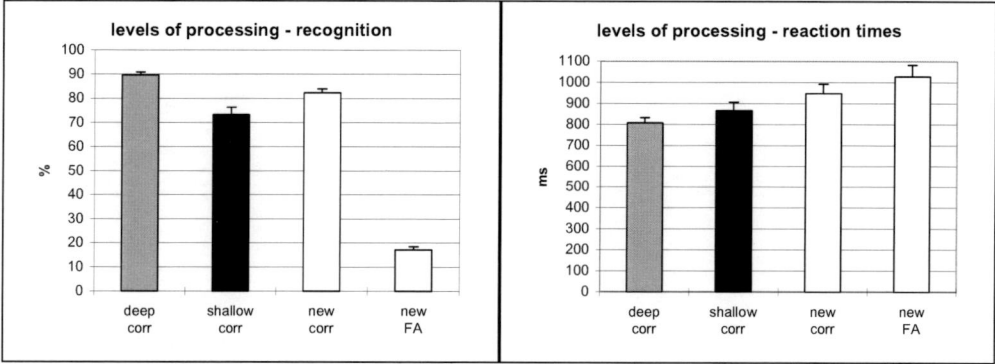

Figure 4.7 Behavioral results obtained in Experiment 2: Recognition rates and false alarm rate in percent of presented items (left side), reaction times (right side); deep = deeply encoded items, shallow = shallowly encoded items, new = new items, corr = correctly recognized, FA = false alarms.

4.2.2 ERP data

Due to high contamination of the EEG with movement-related artifacts (subjects had to respond vocally during the study phase) no reliable ERPs could be obtained in the study phase of Experiment 2. Therefore only ERP data from the recognition test could be analyzed.

Old/new effects for deeply and shallowly encoded words

Fig. 4.8 displays the ERP waveforms at three midline electrodes and at lateral frontal, central and parietal recording sites elicited by old and new items in the recognition test. Starting around 300 ms the waveforms evoked by old items were more positive going than for new items. These old/new effects were observable for recognition of both item types.

Deeply encoded items elicited three temporally and topographically distinct old/new effects. An early phasic, frontal positivity with a maximum at midline electrodes could be observed from 300 to 500 ms. Starting around 450 ms and extending until around 900 ms a parietally distributed phasic positive wave emerged that partially overlapped the early frontal old/new effect. Finally, a sustained positive slow wave was observable most pronounced over right frontal recording sites. This late right frontal old/new effect started at about 800 ms and extended until around 1800 ms post stimulus onset. For recognized items which had

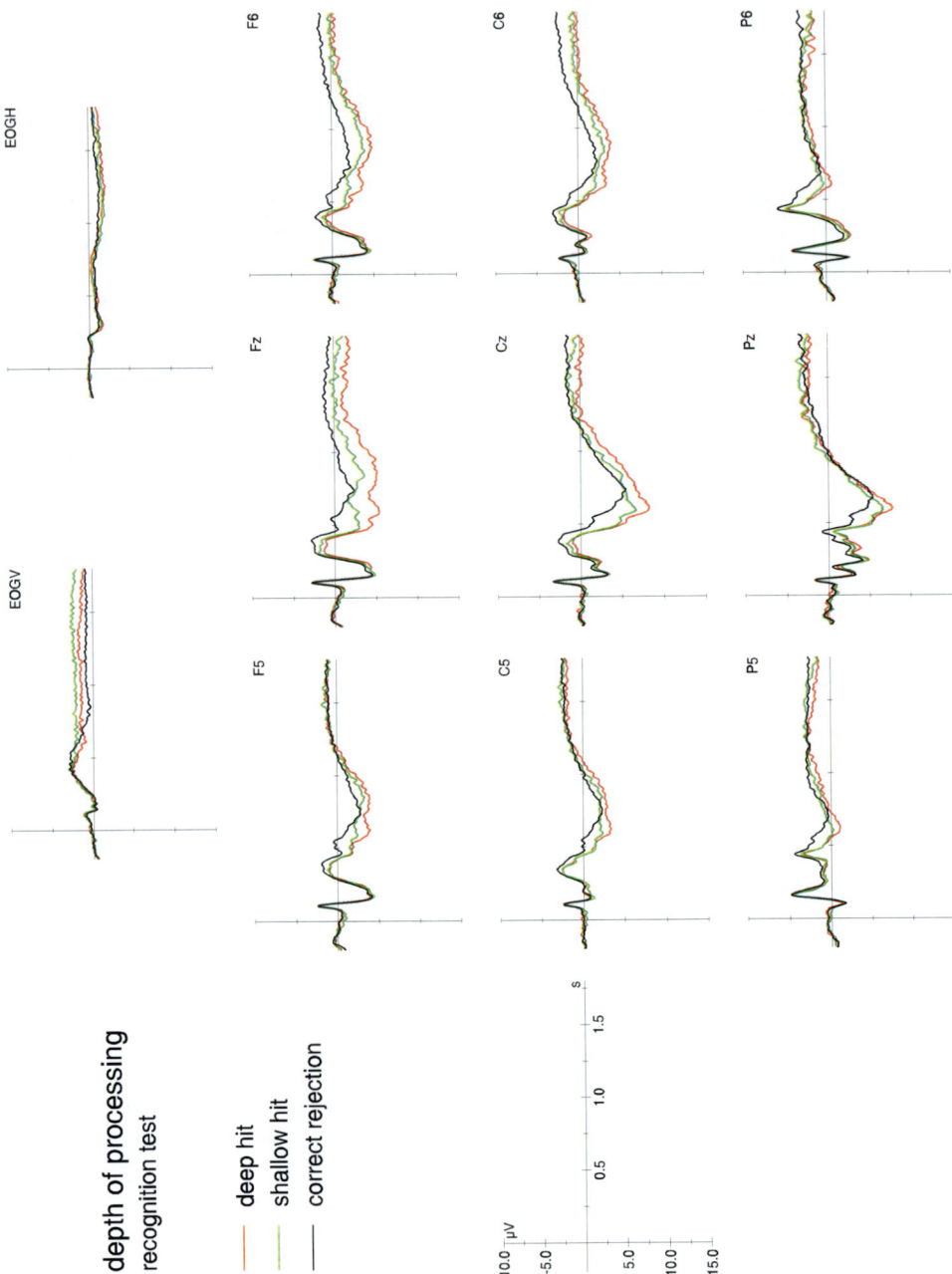

Figure 4.8 ERP waveforms elicited by recognized deeply and shallowly encoded items and by correctly rejected new items and averaged across subjects at recognition test.

undergone shallow encoding a very similar spatio-temporal pattern of old/new effects occurred, but substantially smaller in magnitude.

Though the pattern of the old/new effects evoked by deeply and shallowly encoded old items was topographically similar to the pattern elicited by TBR and TBF items in Experiment 1, the old/new effects particularly at parietal recording sites were substantially smaller and also restricted to a smaller time window than in Experiment 1. To account for this pattern and in order to guarantee maximal comparability with the results of Experiment 1 time windows for mean amplitude quantification were chosen such that the peak of the observable old/new effects was centered in the according window. The time intervals were as follows: early 300-450 ms, middle 450-600 ms, and late 950-1200 ms. However, this selection of time windows does not rule out a partial overlap of the old/new effects in the early and middle time windows.

Table 4.8. Experiment 2: ANOVA results for ERP measures in the recognition test

	df	F-values
I/R type	2, 38	13.09‡
I/R type × time	2, 38	7.67‡
I/R type × time × lat dim	4, 76	5.79‡
I/R type × time × a-p dim	4, 76	3.95**
I/R type × time × a-p dim × lat dim	8, 152	7.83‡
I/R type × lat dim	4, 76	6.69†
I/R type × a-p dim	4, 76	3.41*
I/R type × a-p dim × lat dim	8, 152	8.20‡

I/R type = item/response type (recognized deeply and shallowly encoded items, and correct rejections); time = time window; lat dim = lateral dimension; a-p dim = anterior-posterior dimension;
* = $p < 0.05$; ** = $p < 0.01$; † = $p < 0.005$; ‡ = $p < 0.0005$.

The results of the four-way ANOVA with the factors time window, lateral dimension, anterior-posterior dimension, and item type are displayed in Table 4.8. Based on the interactions time window × item type × lateral dimension × anterior-posterior dimension three-way ANOVAs with the factors response type (2 levels: correctly recognized, new), lateral and anterior-posterior dimensions were performed for each time window and for deeply and shallowly encoded items separately.

In the early time interval for deeply encoded items a main effect of response type ($F(1, 19) = 10.03$, $p < 0.01$), the interaction response type × lateral dimension type ($F(2, 38) = 7.05$, $p < 0.005$), and the triple interaction response type × lateral dimension × anterior-posterior dimension type ($F(4, 76) = 3.05$, $p < 0.05$) were significant. The interactions indicate that the old/new difference was most pronounced over frontocentral midline regions. One-way ANOVAs tests revealed a significant old/new difference for all regions ($ps < 0.05$), except for the left frontal and central regions where the old/new effects were marginally significant ($p = 0.076$ and 0.052, respectively). The highest treatment magnitudes were obtained for the central midline recording sites ($\Omega^2 = 0.39$). The same analysis performed for items which had undergone shallow encoding gave rise to a main effect of response type ($F(1, 19) = 5.80$, $p < 0.05$), and a marginally significant interaction response type × lateral dimension type ($F(2, 38) = 3.20$, $p = 0.067$), suggesting that the old/new differences where most pronounced at midline electrodes.

In the middle time interval for both item types a main effect of response type (deeply encoded words: $F(1, 19) = 36.87$, $p < 0.0001$; shallowly encoded words $F(1, 19) = 18.28$, $p < 0.001$), the interaction response type × lateral dimension type (deeply encoded: $F(2, 38) = 25.02$, $p < 0.0001$; shallowly encoded: $F(2, 38) = 8.92$, $p < 0.001$), and the triple interaction response type × lateral dimension × anterior-posterior dimension type (deeply encoded: $F(4, 76) = 19.59$, $p < 0.0001$; shallowly encoded: $F(4, 76) = 5.16$, $p < 0.01$) were significant. For both item types one-way ANOVAs revealed maximal magnitudes of the old/new differences at frontal and central medial regions (deeply encoded: $\Omega^2 = 0.80$ and 0.77, respectively; shallowly encoded: $\Omega^2 = 0.52$ and 0.58) and a slight lateralization to the left at central and parietal recording sites reflected by an interaction response type × lateral dimension (deeply encoded items: central regions $F(2, 38) = 35.63$, $p < 0.0001$, parietal regions $F(2, 38) = 9.84$, $p < 0.0001$; shallowly encoded items: central regions $F(2, 38) = 18.70$, $p < 0.0005$).

ANOVAs for deeply encoded items in the late time window gave rise to a significant main effect of response type ($F(1, 19) = 16.62$, $p < 0.001$) and significant interactions response type × lateral dimension ($F(2, 38) = 4.33$, $p < 0.05$), response type × anterior-posterior dimension ($F(2, 38) = 11.72$, $p < 0.001$), and the triple interaction response type × lateral dimension × anterior-posterior dimension ($F(4, 76) = 14.87$, $p < 0.0001$). The interactions reflect the fact that old/new differences were significant only at medial and right frontal and central regions ($p < 0.0005$). The highest treatment magnitudes were obtained for the medial frontal and right central regions ($\Omega^2 = 0.61$ and 0.53).

The same analysis conducted on ERP data for shallowly encoded items revealed significant interactions response type × anterior-posterior dimension ($F(2, 38) = 5.77$, $p < 0.05$) and response type × lateral dimension × anterior-posterior dimension ($F(4, 76) = 5.37$, $p < 0.01$). These interactions reflect the fact that the old/new differences were significant at right and medial frontal, and at right central regions ($ps < 0.05$) but not at other regions. The highest treatment magnitude was obtained for the right frontal region ($\Omega^2 = 0.38$).

Between-condition comparison

In order to examine differences between the old/new effects elicited by deeply and shallowly encoded items as in Experiment 1 repeated measures ANOVAs were performed for the ERP difference measures separately for the three time windows and for the two item types. The results of the three-way ANOVAs for the three time windows are displayed in Table 4.9. The differences in the mean amplitude of the frontal and posterior regions between the recognized and new items are illustrated in Fig. 4.9, and the according scalp topographies in the three time windows are displayed in Fig. 4.10. Inspection of Fig. 4.10 suggests that the old/new effects elicited by both item types do not differ topographically in any of the three time windows. However, the magnitude of the old/new effects seems to be larger for deeply encoded items. The topographic maps show that the early frontal and parietal subcomponents overlap in the early and middle time windows. ANOVA of the difference data from the 300-

Table 4.9 ERP difference measures in Exp. 2: ANOVA results for the three time intervals in the recognition test

		F-values		
	df	300-450 ms	450-600 ms	950-1200ms
Item type	1, 19	5.80*	3.88	2.38
Item type × lat dim	2, 38	3.20	2.88	1.27
Item type × a-p dim	2, 38	0.43	2.98	5.77*
Item type × lat dim × a-p dim	4, 76	1.75	4.16*	5.37**

lat dim = lateral dimension; a-p dim = anterior-posterior dimension; $* = p < 0.05$; $** = p < 0.01$.

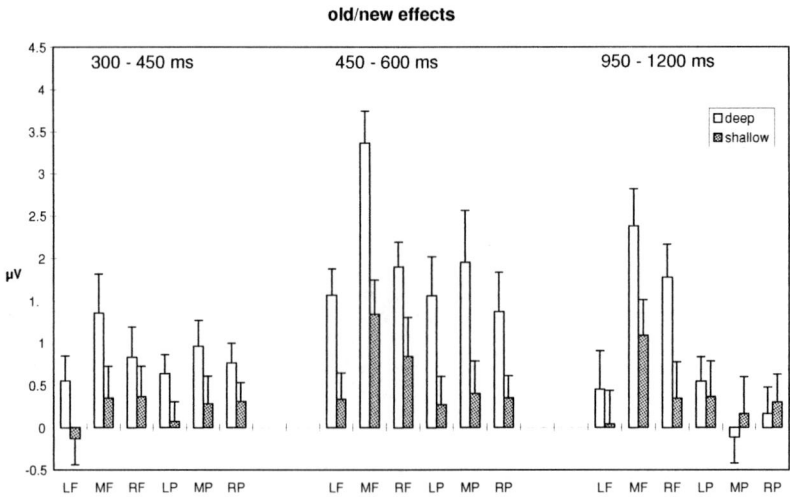

Figure 4.9 Mean difference between the amplitudes of the ERPs elicited by recognized and new items in the 300-550, 450-850, and 950-1200 ms latency regions, shown separately for deeply and shallowly encoded items at frontal (LF, MF, RF) and posterior (LP, MP, RP) recording sites.

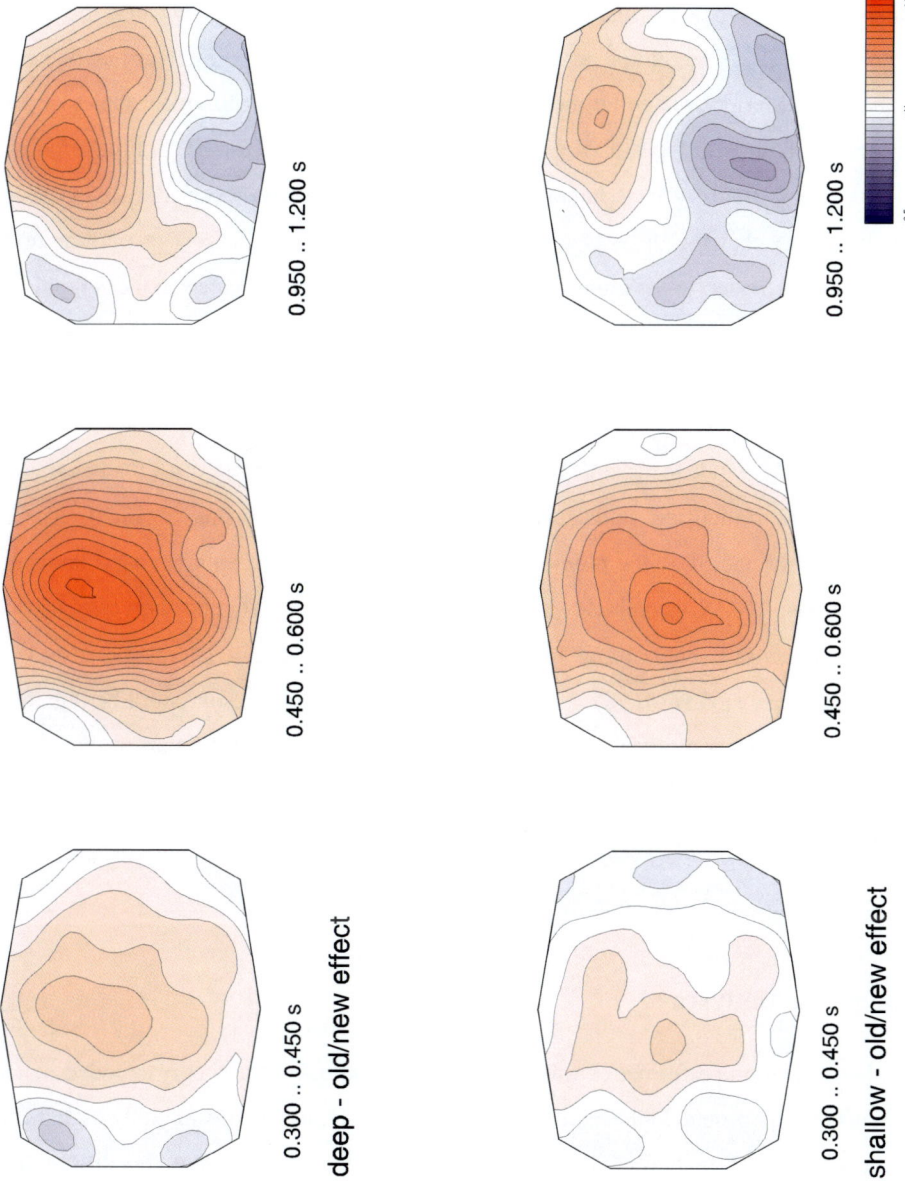

Figure 4.10 Topographic maps of the differences between ERPs for recognized and new items (old/new effects) in three time intervals. Upper row: deeply encoded, lower row: shallowly encoded words.

450 ms latency range revealed a main effect of item type, reflecting the fact that the early frontal old/new effect was larger for deeply encoded items. Because no interactions of item type with anterior-posterior or lateral dimension were significant, the scalp topographies of the old/new effects for both item types do not differ statistically. In the 450-600 ms time window the triple interaction item type × lateral dimension × anterior-posterior dimension was significant, indicating that the difference of the old/new effects was largest at midline and posterior regions. In order to examine whether this interaction indicates a topographical difference, the same ANOVA was conducted on amplitude normalized difference measures. No significant interactions ($p > 0.389$) were found indicating that topographical distributions of the old/new effects did not differ between deeply and shallowly encoded items.

In the late time window the interactions item type × anterior-posterior dimension and item type × lateral dimension and anterior-posterior dimension were obtained. These interactions reflect the fact, that the old/new effects were larger for deeply encoded items at right frontal regions. ANOVA conducted on amplitude normalized difference waves revealed no significant interactions, but a trend for the interaction item type × lateral dimension × anterior-posterior dimension ($F(4, 76) = 2.18, p = 0.093$). This latter result could be due to a partial overlap of the earlier old/new effects for deeply encoded items. In support of this view, the same ANOVAs performed for normalized data in a later time window (1050-1300 ms) revealed no significant interaction ($p = 0.149$).

4.2.3 Subgroup analyses

While recognition performance was on a similarly high level for deeply encoded items and TBR items in Experiment 2 and Experiment 1, respectively, it was substantially higher for shallowly encoded items than for TBF items. Thus, it is conceivable that the differential pattern of old/new effects obtained in Experiment 1 and Experiment 2, rather than reflecting processing differences between depth of encoding and intentional forgetting, are associated with the differential performance pattern between TBF (59 % recognized) and shallowly encoded items (73 % recognized). To address this issue we performed a median split of the participants in Experiment 2 according to their performance levels for shallowly encoded words[8]. Mean hit rate to shallowly encoded words was 83.7 and 62.9% in the high and low recognition group, respectively, suggesting that for the low recognition group the hit rate for shallowly encoded items was similar to the hit rates for TBF items in Experiment 1 (59.2%). The ERP waveforms evoked by new items and shallowly encoded old items in both subgroups are displayed in Figure 4.11. As is apparent from the figure, in the high recognition subgroup the magnitudes of the parietal old/new effects to shallowly encoded items was higher than in the low recognition subgroup, whereas the late right frontal old/new effect was about equal in both groups. In order to test whether the parietal old/new effect is present also in the low recognition subgroup or if this effect is absent similarly as in the directed forgetting study, ANOVAs for the middle time window were performed contrasting correctly recognized shallowly encoded items and new items. It is important to note that due to the smaller number of subjects in the subgroup the statistical power is reduced in this analysis. ANOVA for the low recognition group revealed a marginally significant main effect of item type ($F(1, 9) = 3.75$, $p = 0.0847$), which indicates that the parietal old/new effect was also present for shallowly encoded items even when performance levels were matched with Experiment 1. For the high performance group a significant main effect of item type in the high recognition group ($F(1, 9) = 22.50$, $p < 0.005$) was found. These results indicate that the magnitude of the old/new effect for shallowly encoded items is reduced in the low recognition group as compared to the whole sample of participants and suggest that the magnitude of this effect is affected by recognition performance. However, the marginal significant effect of item type found for shallowly encoded items in the low recognition group is still in contrast to the complete absence of the corresponding effects for TBF items in Experiment 1.

In sum, the foregoing analyses revealed, that recognition of studied items evoked early old/new effects with frontal and centroparietal maxima and a sustained late right frontal old/new difference. These old/new effects were larger in magnitude for items which had undergone deep encoding. However, no topographical differences between the old/new effects elicited by deeply and shallowly encoded words were found in any of the three time intervals.

---

[8] That means, participants with a higher recognition performance for shallowly encoded words than the median recognition rate of all subjects (75 %) belong to the high recognition group, subjects with a lower recognition rate for shallowly encoded items are in the low recognition group.

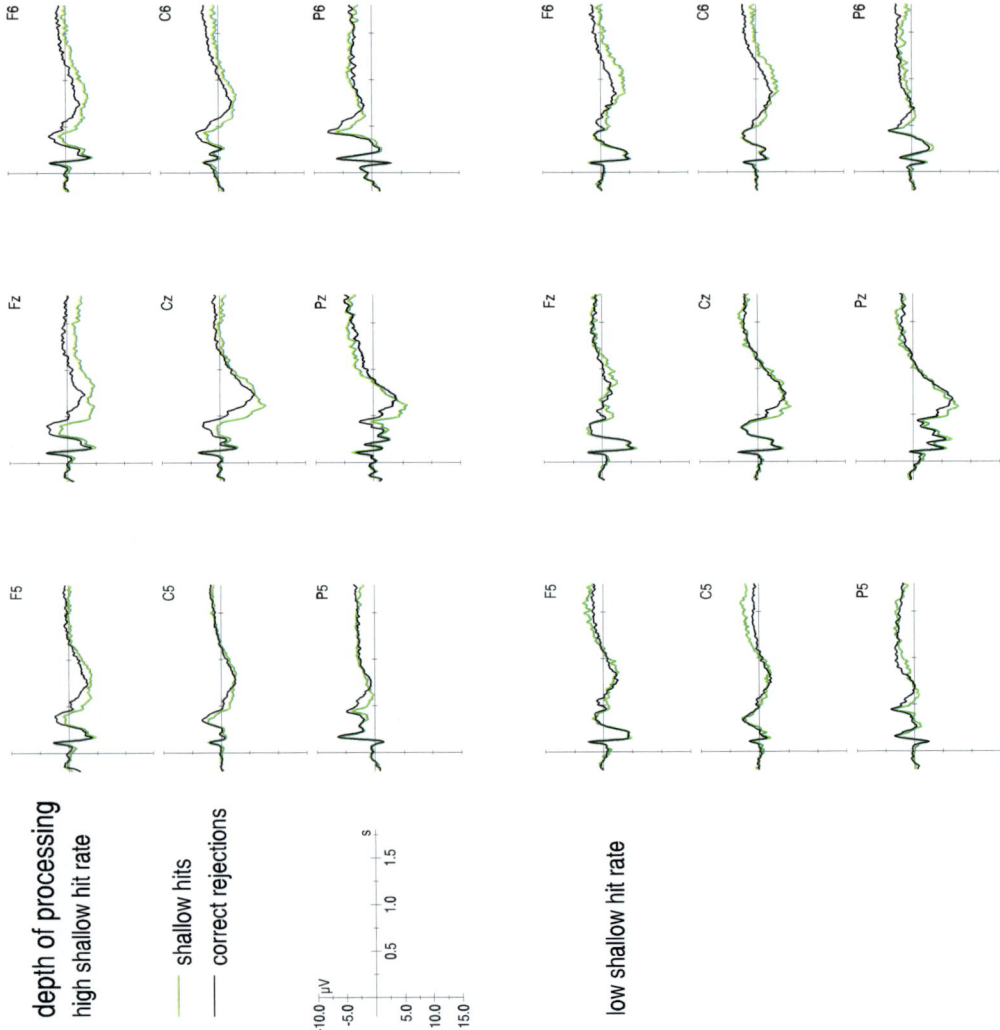

Figure 4.11 ERP waveforms elicited by recognized shallowly encoded items (shallow hits) and correctly rejected new items (correct rejections) averaged across two subgroups of subjects with high and low recognition performance for shallowly studied items, respectively.

Chapter 5

Discussion

5.1 Experiment 1

5.1.1 Study phase

Recording ERPs at the time of the study phase enables the researcher to examine electrical brain activity associated with stimulus evaluation and encoding. In the present study, ERPs were recorded at two instances in the study phase: first, at word presentation, second, when subjects were cued whether to remember or forget the word.

Pre-cue ERPs

ERPs for to-be-forgotten (TBF) words at word presentation revealed a typical subsequent memory effect (SME), i.e., the waveforms for subsequently successfully recognized items were more positive-going than for unrecognized items. The observed SME was parietally distributed and seemed to be a modulation of the P300 component. This SME could be associated with the rote rehearsal (i.e., simple, shallow processing) activity performed by the subjects before they know whether to remember or forget the presented item (cf. Karis et al., 1984; Donchin & Fabiani, 1991 who have shown a modulation of the P300 component at study in subjects employing a rote encoding strategy. See also Section 1.3.2.1). Due to lack of trials, the ERPs to unrecognized TBR items could not be examined in the present study. However, one can assume that the encoding strategies before the presentation of the cue should be the same for both TBR and TBF words. This is supported by the fact, that there is no difference between the ERPs elicited by TBR and TBF words successfully recognized later in the experiment.

Post-cue ERPs

According to the differential encoding model of directed forgetting and to introspective reports of the subjects (in the postexperimental debriefing most subjects reported to stop processing the items when a forget cue was shown, whereas to rehearse and elaborately process the TBR words), processing of the words should start to differ, as soon as the subject was cued whether to remember or forget the particular item. These differences could have their correlates in the ERPs *following the cue* onset. And indeed, the cue seems to have a strong influence on the P300 component, which is a positive ERP component with a centro-parietal maximum elicited around 300-1000 ms after stimulus onset. It is generated for task-relevant events, its amplitude is negatively correlated with the probability of these events and covaries with the amount of information that can be extracted from the events (for an overview see, e.g., Donchin & Coles, 1988). It was postulated that the P300 reflects processes of updating and reorganization in working memory (context updating) which occur when a stimulus is compared with a context-related expectancy (Donchin, 1981; Donchin & Coles, 1988; Mecklinger & Ullsperger, 1993; Ullsperger & Mecklinger, 1996). In the present study, the remember cue evoked a much larger and slightly earlier P300 than the forget cue. This P300 effect cannot be explained by probability differences, because the remember and forget cues were presented with the same probability (50 % each) in randomized order. The P300 component seems to be influenced by the functional relevance of the cue, probably reflecting some updating of rehearsal strategy after the cue.

Moreover, the P300 amplitude seems to be modulated by subsequent memory performance. In other words, after cue presentation a subsequent memory effect was found for TBF words. This can be interpreted as a hint that encoding and rehearsal strategies do not seem to stop immediately, when subjects receive the cue to forget. It appears that at least some TBF items are further processed, a fact which is in contrast to the differential encoding model. However, the question, whether functionally different encoding occurs for TBF and TBR items cannot be addressed directly. This could only be done, if the spatio-temporal distribution of the SMEs for TBR and TBF items could be compared, which is not possible due to the lack of ERP data for one condition (unrecognized TBR items).

Taken together, in the study phase some of the ERP data are consistent with the differential encoding model, while others do not support it, but the results do not suffice to draw more detailed inferences about the mechanisms involved in directed forgetting. A thorough analysis of the data acquired in the recognition test phase is necessary to disclose the cognitive processes involved in intentional forgetting.

5.1.2 Recognition test

Behavioral data of Experiment 1 showed that cueing participants either to remember or to forget presented items resulted in a significantly lower recognition rate of TBF items compared with TBR items, indicating that the employed paradigm led to the expected directed forgetting effect. Furthermore, the recognition-related ERPs differed qualitatively as well as quantitatively between TBR and TBF words, suggesting that the instruction to remember did not lead to solely stronger memory traces than the instruction to forget items but rather is associated with differential brain activation patterns at retrieval. With respect to the hypotheses, the differential encoding and alternative models of single-item-cued directed forgetting will be discussed next.

The ERP findings are consistent with the predictions based on the *differential encoding* model only to a certain extent. In the hypotheses it was noted that TBR and TBF words should have the same familiarity, thus the early frontal old/new effect should be of the same magnitude for both item types. However, the early frontally distributed old/new effects are lower in amplitude for TBF than for TBR items. This finding can be interpreted in three ways: first, familiarity is (contrary to the findings of Gardiner, 1994, and Basden & Basden, 1996) sensitive to the directed forgetting effect; second, the early time window did not capture only the early frontal but also some other overlapping and memory trace dependent components of the old/new effect; or third, the early frontal old/new effect does not only reflect familiarity, but is also influenced by other processes. A further discussion of this issue can be found in the General discussion (Section 5.3).

If solely differential encoding was responsible for the observed directed forgetting effect, the lower strength of the memory traces of TBF items should have led to a lower magnitude of the parietal old/new effect. However, the parietal component is not only diminished but it is virtually absent for TBF items. This result was confirmed by the topographical analysis showing that the scalp distributions of the old/new effects in the 550-850 ms latency range differed between TBR and TBF items. One explanation could be that the absence of the parietal old/new effect in recognition of TBF items results from a weaker memory trace of those items leading to a lower proportion of consciously recollected items and a lower recollection rate for TBF items ('dilution effect'). This interpretation would be consistent with the finding by Basden and Basden (1996, Experiment 3) who have shown with a remember/know procedure (Tulving, 1985) that the instruction to forget leads to a substantial reduction of conscious recollection.

The finding that the late right frontal old/new effect is larger for TBF items than for TBR words suggests that post-retrieval processes for both item types differ at least quantitatively. However, this result is in contrast to the prediction that for TBF items should be retrieved less contextual information and thus the late right frontal old/new effect should be lower. An alternative interpretation could be as follows. Given that the late right frontal old/new effect is associated with retrieval effort and source monitoring (Wilding & Rugg, 1996) it is conceivable that items with a weaker memory trace, i. e. TBF words, require more retrieval effort and that this is reflected by the higher amplitudes of the late right frontal old/new effect. From this viewpoint the data could be consistent with the differential encoding model of item-by-item directed forgetting.

Conversely, if the directed forgetting effects resulted at least partly from *retrieval inhibition*, larger retrieval effort would be necessary to release TBF items from inhibition (Geiselman & Bagheri, 1985; MacLeod, 1989). It is conceivable, that a higher activation level of structures involved in retrieval is required to overcome retrieval inhibition and that this is reflected by the higher magnitude of the old/new effects, particularly of the right frontal effect.

From these considerations it follows that the ERP data from Experiment 1 do not unequivocally support either model of directed forgetting. Especially the interpretations of the findings about the late right frontal old/new effect are equivocal. Therefore the second experiment was conducted to examine the influence of differential encoding on recognition-related ERP old/new effects directly.

5.2 Experiment 2 - recognition test

Behavioral data revealed that the instruction to encode words either deeply or shallowly led to a significantly lower recognition performance and slower reaction times for the items which had undergone shallow processing. In other words, also the levels-of-processing manipulation was successful, thus making Experiment 2 comparable to the directed forgetting experiment. However, compared to the recognition rate of TBF items in Experiment 1 more shallowly encoded words were recognized. Therefore, a subgroup analysis of the ERP data was performed for those participants whose recognition performance in Experiment 2 matched the performance of the subjects in Experiment 1. The ERP effects in this subgroup were weaker but showed the same patterns as in the entire group.

Recognition of deeply encoded words elicited early old/new effects with frontal and parietal maxima and a late right frontal positive slow wave. Interestingly, the shallowly encoded words evoked recognition-related old/new effects with the same topographical and temporal distribution, but a smaller magnitude. These findings are consistent with the view that recognition of both item types activate the same brain structures, but to a different extent. The early old/new effects in the time range from 300 to 600 ms, covered by the first two time windows, were smaller in magnitude for shallowly encoded items. This result replicates similar findings by other groups (Paller & Kutas, 1992; Rugg et al., 1998b), and it is consistent with the notion that a weaker memory trace leads to a lower amplitude of the old/new effect. In contrast to Rugg et al. (1998b), in our experiment also the early frontal old/new effect between 300 and 450 ms was influenced by the manipulation of depth of encoding. Similarly to the findings for the early frontal old/new effects in Experiment 1, this result is inconsistent with the notion that the encoding condition should not influence the amount of familiarity (Gardiner, 1988) which is reflected by this component of the old/new effect.

Moreover, similarly as in Experiment 1, the reduction of the parietal old/new effect could also partly reflect a lower conscious recollection rate for shallowly encoded compared with deeply encoded items (Gardiner, 1988). However, in contrast to Experiment 1, the parietal old/new effect is not entirely absent for shallowly encoded words even in the subgroup with low recognition rates for those items.

The right frontal old/new effect was similar for both item types, with a slightly lower magnitude for shallowly encoded items. This finding is consistent with the view that the right frontal old/new effect reflects post-retrieval processes (Allan et al., 1998; Wilding & Rugg, 1996), which should be reduced for shallowly encoded words, rather than retrieval effort, which should be higher for shallowly encoded items.

Taken together, in this experiment hypotheses about the old/new effects were confirmed with the exception of the early frontal effect. In the following section, the results of both experiments will be compared in order to draw inferences about the mechanisms underlying directed forgetting.

5.3 General discussion

Intentional forgetting is an important function of healthy human memory for goal-oriented actions. It is essential for suppression of irrelevant information which could interfere with current goal-relevant information. Investigation of intentional forgetting has been performed with the directed forgetting paradigm for several decades (MacLeod, 1998). It was found that the directed forgetting instruction impairs the memory performance for to-be-forgotten (TBF) information and reduces proactive interference from TBF items on subsequently studied material. While there is consensus among most researchers about the mechanisms of directed forgetting in the list method (mainly retrieval inhibition) (e.g., Basden & Basden, 1998, MacLeod, 1998), it is still at issue which psychological and psychophysiological mechanisms underlie directed forgetting in the item method. Many researchers tend to explain the directed forgetting effect in the item procedure by differential encoding, i.e., selective rehearsal and deep processing of TBR items compared to only shallow processing of TBF items (e.g., Basden & Basden, 1998; H. Johnson, 1994; Wilson & Kipp, 1998). However, several studies have revealed results which are not consistent with the differential encoding model alone, but provide support for the hypothesis that retrieval inhibition plays an important role also in item method directed forgetting (e.g., Geiselman & Bagheri, 1985; MacLeod, 1989). This means that TBF items are encoded, too, but the instruction to forget prevents these items from being recovered at retrieval. These TBF items can apparently be released from inhibition, e.g., by second presentation in a study list (Geiselman & Bagheri, 1985).

The aim of the present study was to address the issue if differential encoding alone or differential encoding and additional retrieval inhibition underlie the lower memory performance in a single-item-cueing directed forgetting task. This was achieved by combined behavioral and event-related potential measurements. ERPs are well suited for this investigation because of their high temporal resolution and their process-specific spatio-temporal distributions. Two experiments were conducted in which participants were instructed to either remember or forget words (Experiment 1), or to deeply or shallowly process the items (Experiment 2). The main rationale was the following: Under the assumption that in both experiments the mechanism separating remembering from forgetting and deep from shallow processing is the same, namely differential encoding, the spatio-temporal patterns of the ERP effects obtained in both experiment should not differ. In contrast, differences in ERP patterns between both experiments would suggest, that at least partially differential cognitive processes are involved in word recognition in a directed forgetting paradigm compared to a levels-of-processing manipulation (see Chapter 3).

Behavioral measures

The behavioral results of both experiments were similar: the recognition rate for TBR items and deeply encoded items as well as the correct rejection rates and false alarm rates were highly similar in both experiments. Moreover, both manipulations lead to a significantly lower recognition performance for TBF items and shallowly encoded words, respectively. However, the performance was lower for TBF items than for shallowly encoded words.

In sum, both experimental manipulations lead to similar behavioral effects. Comparison of the spatio-temporal ERP patterns in both experiments will reveal whether the same or different neuronal processes underlie the lower memory performance for TBF and shallowly encoded items.

CHAPTER 5. DISCUSSION

ERP measures

As stated in Section 5.1.1, the ERP data from the study phase in Experiment 1 are partly consistent with differential encoding as well as with retrieval inhibition. The results indicate that processing of TBR and TBF items is similar before cue presentation and differs in the post-cue interval. The finding of a subsequent memory effect for TBF items in the post-cue interval suggests that these items are further processed and encoded although subjects know that they are to-be-forgotten. The data do not allow to unequivocally disentangle both models of directed forgetting, therefore, the general discussion will focus on the recognition-related ERPs from both experiments.

The patterns of ERP old/new effects in the two studies differed in several ways. A summary of the pattern of old/new effects is illustrated in Table 5.1. As apparent from the table and as already discussed in the previous sections, the results did not confirm all hypotheses.

Table 5.1. Patterns of mean differences of ERP amplitudes elicited by recognized and new items (old/new effects) in both experiments (+/++: large/very large old/new effect, -: no old/new effect)

	directed forgetting		depth of processing	
	to-be-remembered	to-be-forgotten	deeply encoded	shallowly encoded
early midfrontal effect	++ >	+	++ >	+
parietal effect	++	-	++ >	+
late right frontal effect	+ <	++	++ >	+(+)

Before turning to the implications about the mechanisms underlying directed forgetting, the results for the early frontal old/new effect will be discussed briefly. The early frontal old/new effect was proposed to reflect familiarity, i.e., facilitated access to conceptual and/or lexical information (e.g., Rugg et al., 1998b; Mecklinger et al., 1999; Penney et al.,

1999). For both experiments it was hypothesized on the basis of the results of several psychological investigations (Gardiner, 1988; Gardiner et al., 1994; Basden & Basden, 1996) that the item types should not differ in their respective familiarity and therefore evoke similar early frontal old/new effects. However, contrary to the hypotheses, the early frontal old/new effect was reduced for TBF and shallowly encoded items. These results indicate that the amount of familiarity is modulated by the directed forgetting procedure as well as by levels of processing manipulations. On the other hand, one could speculate that the early frontal effect itself consists of several overlapping subcomponents, one of which only is associated to familiarity. In the present study, the early frontal old/new effect could be overlapped by a second subcomponent, which is sensitive to a depth of processing manipulation, e.g., to the strength of memory trace.

Comparison of the old/new effects in Experiments 1 and 2

While directed forgetting led to qualitative as well as quantitative differences between the old/new effects elicited by TBR and TBF items, respectively, manipulating the depth of processing gave rise only to a quantitative difference between the old/new effects evoked by deeply and shallowly encoded words in all three time intervals. This view can be derived from the fact that the parietally focused old/new effects were virtually absent for TBF items but only reduced in magnitude for shallowly encoded items. This differential pattern of results was still present when performance for TBF items and shallowly encoded items were equated. The view that the parietal old/new effects differ only quantitatively between deeply and shallowly encoded words but not between TBR and TBF items is also supported by the analysis of the topographical profiles of the old/new effects in both experiments. This analysis revealed a statistically indistinguishable scalp topography for the old/new effects evoked by deeply and shallowly encoded items, whereas there were topographical differences of the old/new effects in the time range of the parietal old/new effect between TBR and TBF items even when the topographical profiles were rescaled to remove amplitude differences between the contrasted conditions (R. Johnson, 1993). Based on this pattern of results obtained for the early old/new effects, it is conceivable that the amount of consciously recollected items was reduced after shallow encoding relative to deep encoding, whereas qualitatively different retrieval operations were evoked for TBF relative to TBR items. A hint on the nature of the differential retrieval operations for TBF and TBR items can be inferred from the ERPs effects obtained in the late time intervals. The late right frontal old/new effect was greater in magnitude for TBF items compared to TBR words. The depth of processing manipulation lead to a reversed pattern of the late right frontal old/new effect with smaller magnitudes for shallowly encoded words. That means, the directed forgetting instruction has influenced retrieval processes in a different way than the levels-of-processing manipulation in the early time intervals as well as in the post-response period. According to the main rationale of this study, these results suggest that differential encoding *alone* cannot account for the effects of directed forgetting. They are more consistent with the view that items followed by the instruction to forget become inhibited and less accessible, and thus more difficult to retrieve (Geiselman & Bagheri, 1985; MacLeod, 1989). With respect to the middle latency range, the most intriguing result is the absence of the parietal old/new effect in recognition of TBF items. Given that the parietal old/new effect is a correlate of conscious recollection (see Section 1.3.2.2), its absence indicates that recognition of TBF items was more familiarity-based than recognition of TBR items. It can be speculated that the absence of the parietal old/new effect could be an indirect sign of retrieval inhibition of TBF items. It appears that the brain structures which mediate the parietal old/new effect for TBR items were not active when TBR items were to be recognized. Thus, speculating further, retrieval inhibition could be understood as hindering brain structures necessary for conscious recollection to become active.

An interesting question concerns the functional significance of the late right frontal slow wave elicited by TBF items. It could be argued that it reflects post-retrieval evaluation processes, like the reconstruction of the study context. While responses to TBR items might have been given with high confidence, there might have been more response uncertainty for TBF items that led to larger demands on post-retrieval rechecking and evaluation processes. This interpretation, however seems rather unlikely, because similar arguments would be true for shallowly encoded items. Given that uncertainty about contextual information from the study episode and resulting additional search effort would be reflected in a higher amplitude of the late right frontal old/new effect, shallowly encoded items should evoke a higher amplitude for this effect, too, which was not the case in the present study.

Another, more likely interpretation could be the following: TBF words which were retrieved must have been released from retrieval inhibition. In fact, the instruction for the recognition test (subjects have to designate TBR words as well as TBF words as 'old') changes the functional significance of TBF items. As long as participants do not know the instructions for the final recognition test, TBF items are treated as irrelevant information, but they become relevant for performance in the recognition test itself. Therefore, a reorganization of memory for the presented TBF items and their contextual information seems necessary. According to Bjork (1989) retrieval of TBF items is blocked by increased activation of TBR items. Retrieval of TBF items necessitates a deblocking or release from inhibition of the access routes to these items. It could be speculated that the higher amplitude of the late right frontal old/new effect reflects this release from inhibition and that this process extends beyond the subjects response. Recent ERP studies of recognition memory have reported not only a right frontal but also medial and left frontal ERP effects in the late latency region beginning around 700 ms which seemed to be related to retrieval strategies (Senkfor & Van Petten, 1998; Ranganath & Paller, 1999). These findings indicate that late frontal ERP effects in recognition tasks are no unitary entity but a heterogeneous phenomenon reflecting different forms of control and evaluation processes associated with memory retrieval. The present results, however, indicate that one form of control operations reflected by late frontal slow waves in explicit retrieval tasks is the release from inhibition for intentionally forgotten items. Further research will be necessary to disentangle these different kinds of processes and to relate the electrophysiological findings to the results of functional brain imaging studies (Rugg et al., 1998a; Wagner et al., 1998a).

Conclusion

The present results suggest that in single-item-cued directed forgetting retrieval inhibition plays an important role for the observed performance differences. It is now possible to answer the question which was addressed by the present study - *differential encoding alone* or *differential encoding plus retrieval inhibition*. The results are consistent with the view that multiple processes acting not only on encoding but also on retrieval contribute to the directed forgetting phenomena. Considering the relevant literature, this is the first study using ERP measures to demonstrate the contribution of retrieval inhibition to the directed forgetting effects. Two ERP findings are candidates to - at least indirectly - reflect processes related to retrieval inhibition and release from inhibition: the absence of the parietal old/new effect and the higher amplitude of the late right frontal old/new effect for TBF words, respectively.

5.4 Future research, clinical implications

The present study has demonstrated that retrieval inhibition takes place in item method directed forgetting. Thus, the directed forgetting paradigm can be used as a model for further examinations of these inhibitory processes in memory. It should be noted that the single-item-cueing method is especially well suited for investigations employing event-related study designs (such as ERP and event-related fMRI).

Furthermore, the results of this study provide additional support for the notion that the frontal lobes have an important function in retrieval control and post-retrieval evaluation processes. As reviewed by Shimamura (1995; see also Schacter, 1987; Stuss et al., 1994), lesions of prefrontal cortex can result in impairments of free recall, memory for temporal context, source memory and metamemory (i.e., the ability to make predictions about one's own memory ability). Moreover, patients with frontal lobe lesions are more susceptible to proactive interference (Shimamura et al., 1995). Shimamura (1995) suggested that lesions of prefrontal cortex can disrupt retrieval strategies. From this point of view, it is not surprising that the ERP effects which are assumed to be correlates of memory search, retrieval strategies, and post-retrieval evaluation processes have been found over frontal recording sites (e.g., Rugg et al., 1998c; Senkfor & Van Petten, 1998; Mecklinger, 1998; Mecklinger et al., 1999; Ranganath & Paller, 1999)[9]. In the present study, for example, the larger right frontal old/new effect for TBF items is the most compelling evidence for retrieval inhibition. Shimamura (1995) further proposed that "a general deficit that appears to be indicative of many aspects of

---

[9] As already noted in Section 1.3.1.1, several authors have argued that the generating structures of slow waves are located below the recording sites (e.g., Somjen, 1973; Lang et al., 1988), thus, the frontal slow potentials could most probably be generated in the prefrontal cortex. It is important to note, however, that volume conduction leads to ambiguities with respect to intracranial sources of scalp recorded ERPs (see Chapter 1.3.1).

frontal lobe dysfunction is the failure of these patients to disregard or inhibit irrelevant information" (p. 810).

Based on these considerations, new questions for further research can be raised: How can the directed forgetting paradigm be used to gather more knowledge about frontal lobes and memory functions? Can the method be applied to answer questions in clinical research? More specifically, future studies could have several aims:

(1) The use of the directed forgetting paradigm to investigate subprocesses in long-term memory. Here, the encoding phase is of particular interest. It would be worth to investigate, whether encoding of TBR and TBF words differs qualitatively (thus possibly creating the basis of retrieval inhibition). This could be done by comparing the subsequent memory effects after cue presentation. The methodological problem here is to obtain sufficient trial numbers for all conditions. A possible way would be to perform a final recall test for TBR and TBF words instead of recognition. The directed forgetting paradigm should also be investigated with functional brain imaging, in order to learn more about the functional neuroanatomy of differential encoding and retrieval inhibition processes.

(2) Further characterization of the inhibitory processes probably involved in directed forgetting. The following question would be of high importance: is the late right frontal old/new effect a correlate of retrieval inhibition itself, or is it rather associated with the release from inhibition of TBF items and the resulting reorganization of memory? More experimentation is needed to answer this question. One way could perhaps be using a paradigm similar to that of Geiselman and Bagheri (1985) employing ERP measures.

(3) More research is also needed to find a global concept of the functional significance of recognition-related late frontal ERP effects and frontal activations in functional brain imaging. It is important to find similarities and links between the different studies. Is it always the same kind of process that is reflected in the late frontal ERP effects found by e.g., Rugg et al. (1998c), Senkfor & Van Petten (1998), Mecklinger (1998), Mecklinger et al. (1999), Ranganath & Paller (1999), and in the present study? Could inhibitory

gating or filtering (i.e., the inhibition of irrelevant memories, irrelevant retrieval strategies, irrelevant inputs from posterior cortices etc.) be the global link that explains frontal lobe involvement not only in memory functions but other cognitive functions as well, as proposed by Shimamura (Shimamura, 1995; Shimamura et al., 1995)? It should be tested whether different topographies of frontal slow waves can be found for different control and evaluation processes, and how these processes differ.

(4) Is the directed forgetting paradigm applicable to clinical research? It could be used as a model of inhibitory processes in retrieval from long term memory. Studies of directed forgetting in elderly people have been reported by Zacks et al. (1996), showing a reduced ability to inhibit irrelevant (TBF) material. It would certainly be rewarding to investigate directed forgetting in diseases and lesions where an inhibition deficit for irrelevant information can be expected. This could be, for instance, schizophrenia or - as mentioned above - frontal lobe lesions. It should be examined whether ERP studies of directed forgetting in patients can help in diagnosis of frontal lobe dysfunctions. Directed forgetting studies in combination with ERP measurement might be useful for quantification of the ability to inhibit irrelevant information. It could be hypothesized that frontal lobe lesions result in a lower directed forgetting effect. Is the magnitude of the late right frontal old/new effect in frontal lobe patients lower than in healthy subjects, and is there still a difference between the old/new effects elicited by TBR and TBF items? Where must be a lesion located in prefrontal cortex to impair the ability of intentional forgetting?

(5) One could also speculate that the directed forgetting procedure could help to reveal individual differences between subjects. It is conceivable that subjects with a high reading span can suppress irrelevant information more effectively. Do they also show a higher directed forgetting effect?

(6) Integration of the electrophysiological results with the pharmacological findings of Müller and colleagues (Müller & Mecklinger, 1998; see also Section 1.1.2.2). The pharmacological study could be combined with ERP recording. If, as proposed by Müller

and colleagues, the prefrontal dopamine level is crucial for inhibition of irrelevant information, the following results might be expected: pretreatment with a dopamine antagonist (sulpiride) should lead to a reduced directed forgetting effect (i.e., more TBF items should be recognized), moreover, the amplitude of the late right frontal effect for TBF words should be smaller. If then a dopamine agonist (pergolide) is administered, the directed forgetting effect and the late right frontal old/new effect should be raised again. It would be interesting to prove whether there is a correlation between the difference of the ERPs for recognized TBR and TBF words and the dopaminergic stimulation.

Similarly, patient studies of directed forgetting using the ERP technique could help to understand the influence of dopamine on inhibitory processes. In schizophrenic patients the ability to inhibit irrelevant information should be reduced, thus the recognition rate of TBF words should be higher - relatively closer to the recognition rate of TBR words. ERPs would give more detailed information whether retrieval inhibition is affected in these patients. Also patients with a dopamine deficit, e.g., caused by Parkinson's disease, should exhibit specific changes in behavioral and ERP measures. *De novo* patients and patients off medication would be expected to have a reduced directed forgetting effect, which should increase after medication with L-DOPA or dopamine agonists. The ERP correlates (especially the late right frontal old/new effect) should behave similarly.

This short outlook, as well as the present study should have demonstrated that directed forgetting is a paradigm suitable not only for cognitive neuroscience but also for clinical research. Many new and interesting questions that can be examined with the directed forgetting paradigm have emerged. I am convinced that directed forgetting will continue to play an important role in memory research and will also be applied to clinical studies, maybe it will even be helpful in neuropsychological diagnostics.

Appendix

verbal stimulus material used in both experiments: 360 categorized German nouns

ein Edelstein

Diamant
Rubin
Smaragd
Saphir
Opal
Brillant
Amethyst
Bernstein
Türkis
Topas

ein Familienangehöriger

Opa
Cousine
Neffe
Nichte
Sohn
Tochter
Enkel
Kind
Schwager
Vetter

ein Metall

Kupfer
Gold
Stahl
Blei
Zink
Platin
Magnesium
Nickel
Chrom
Titan

ein Kleidungsstück

Hemd
Rock
Pullover
Bluse
Kleid
Mantel
Schal
Mütze
Hut
Weste

ein Brennstoff

Kohle
Öl
Gas
Benzin
Diesel
Brikett
Spiritus
Alkohol
Petroleum
Kerosin

ein Möbelstück

Sessel
Bett
Sofa
Regal
Kommode
Hocker
Lampe
Liege
Vitrine
Anrichte

ein Wohngebäude

Haus
Hütte
Villa
Zelt
Hotel
Bungalow
Schloß
Wohnung
Palast
Laube

ein alkoholisches Getränk

Sekt
Schnaps
Whiskey
Likör
Wodka
Rum
Gin
Champagner
Weinbrand
Sherry

ein Werkzeug

Zange
Säge
Schraubenzieher
Feile
Bohrer
Meißel
Hobel
Schere
Nagel
Beil

etwas, das/worin man lesen kann

Buch
Zeitung
Heft
Journal
Magazin
Brief
Broschüre
Roman
Comic
Prospekt

ein kirchliches Amt/Beruf

Papst
Bischof
Pastor
Nonne
Abt
Mönch
Kardinal
Vikar
Diakon
Küster

ein militärischer Rang

General
Leutnant
Major
Soldat
Oberst
Feldwebel
Hauptmann
Admiral
Rekrut
Marschall

ein Körperteil	ein Gewürz	eine Frucht
Nase	Oregano	Orange
Ohren	Basilikum	Pflaume
Hals	Curry	Ananas
Augen	Majoran	Erdbeere
Bauch	Kümmel	Mango
Mund	Zimt	Pfirsich
Knie	Muskat	Mandarine
Brust	Knoblauch	Melone
Rumpf	Anis	Zitrone
Rücken	Thymian	Aprikose

ein Säugetier	ein Beruf	eine natürliche Landschaft
Schwein	Lehrer	Wald
Kuh	Arzt	Wiese
Pferd	Maurer	See
Elefant	Verkäufer	Gebirge
Delphin	Maler	Meer
Affe	Bäcker	Wüste
Ratte	Tischler	Tal
Hase	Friseur	Fluß
Giraffe	Elektriker,	Feld
Esel	Klempner	Steppe

eine Waffe	ein Musikinstrument	eine Vogelart
Pistole	Trompete	Amsel
Gewehr	Oboe	Spatz
Schwert	Trommel	Meise
Degen	Tuba	Adler
Kanone	Klarinette	Elster
Dolch	Violine	Taube
Revolver	Saxophon	Rabe
Säbel	Posaune	Papagei
Armbrust	Cello	Storch
Speer	Harfe	Specht

ein Küchengeraät	ein Spielzeug	ein Insekt
Mixer	Puppe	Mücke
Messer	Ball	Wespe
Topf	Teddy	Ameise
Herd	Bausteine	Hummel
Löffel	Puzzle	Käfer
Gabel	Kreisel	Hornisse
Toaster	Dreirad	Spinne
Quirl	Springseil	Libelle
Pfanne	Rassel	Kakerlake
Sieb	Würfel	Moskito

eine Sportart	ein Wetterphänomen	ein Toilettenartikel
Fußball	Sturm	Seife
Schwimmen	Hagel	Klopapier
Tennis	Schnee	Zahnpasta
Handball	Blitz	Creme
Boxen	Sonne	Deodorant
Laufen	Donner	Bürste
Reiten	Orkan	Duschbad
Joggen	Wind	Parfüm
Badminton	Nebel	Handtuch
Radfahren	Wolken	Kamm

ein nichtalkoholisches Getränk	ein Fahrzeug	eine Gemüseart
Tee	Fahrrad	Gurke
Limonade	Bus	Möhre
Kaffee	Motorrad	Brokkoli
Milch	Zug	Erbse
Kakao	Moped	Kohlrabi
Apfelsaft	Flugzeug	Salat
Brause	Schiff	Bohne
Tonic	Mofa	Kartoffel
Cappuccino	Traktor	Zucchini
Sprudel	Kutsche	Spargel

eine Blume	ein Baum	ein Fisch
Tulpe	Buche	Aal
Nelke	Fichte	Hai
Narzisse	Birke	Hecht
Aster	Linde	Hering
Veilchen	Erle	Lachs
Gerbera	Lärche	Barsch
Margarite	Esche	Flunder
Lilie	Pappel	Makrele
Orchidee	Eibe	Scholle
Dahlie	Ulme	Stichling

ein Gebäudeteil	eine Fußbekleidung	ein Schreibgerät
Fenster	Schuh	Füller
Keller	Sandale	Buntstift
Balkon	Socke	Feder
Treppe	Strumpf	Fineliner
Zimmer	Pumps	Filzstift
Flur	Pantoffel	Pinsel
Eingang	Stiefelette	Kugelschreiber
Erker	Latschen	Kreide
Boden	Boots	Textmarker
Etage	Slipper	Griffel

Zusammenfassung der Arbeit

Dissertation zur Erlangung des akademischen Grades Dr. med.

The role of retrieval inhibition in directed forgetting - an event-related brain potential analysis

(Die Rolle der Hemmung des Gedächtnisabrufs beim intentionalen Vergessen - eine Analyse ereigniskorrelierter Hirnpotentiale)

eingereicht von

Markus Ullsperger

angefertigt am

Max-Planck-Institut für neuropsychologische Forschung, Leipzig

betreut von

Prof. Dr. med. D. Y. von Cramon

Juli, 1999

Hintergrund der Untersuchung

Zu den Gedächtnisstörungen gehören nicht nur der Verlust von Gedächtnisinhalten und die Behinderung der Abspeicherung neuer Informationen, sondern auch die Interferenz irrelevanter mit relevanten Informationen. Klinische Studien belegten, daß mit zunehmendem Alter oder bei Läsionen des Frontalhirns die Unterdrückung irrelevanter Gedächtnisinhalte gestört ist (Zacks et al., 1996; Shimamura, 1995). Die Unterdrückung von irrelevanten Gedächtnisinhalten ist außerordentlich wichtig für das zielgerichtete Handeln. Würden weiterhin Informationen abgerufen, die falsch oder inzwischen irrelevant sind, dann käme es durch Interferenzen mit neueren, relevanten Informationen zu einer Beeinträchtigung des Handelns. Daher ist das Vergessen nicht immer als negatives, unerwünschtes Phänomen des menschlichen Gedächtnisses zu werten. Im Gegenteil: das Vergessen bestimmter Informationen ist ein wichtiger Bestandteil des gesunden Gedächtnisses.

Dieses Vergessen irrelevanter Gedächtnisinhalte wird seit etwa 30 Jahren mit dem Paradigma des intentionalen Vergessens (*directed forgetting*) untersucht. Dabei wird den Probanden zumeist verbales Material zum Studium präsentiert. Ein Teil der präsentierten Wörter wird dann als irrelevant bezeichnet, und die Probanden werden aufgefordert, diese Wörter wieder zu vergessen. Es werden zwei Hauptformen des Paradigmas unterschieden. Bei der Listenmethode wird zunächst eine erste Wortliste zum Lernen präsentiert, gefolgt von dem Hinweis, daß diese Liste später irrelevant sei und vergessen werden soll. Danach wird eine zweite (zu merkende) Wortliste präsentiert. Im Gegensatz dazu werden bei der Wortmethode die Wörter einzeln präsentiert, jeweils gefolgt von einem Hinweis, ob dieses Wort zu merken oder zu vergessen ist. Bei beiden Methoden läßt sich im anschließenden Gedächtnistest, bei dem sowohl zu merkende als auch zu vergessende Wörter geprüft werden, eine deutlich reduzierte Gedächtnisleistung für die zu vergessenden Wörter nachweisen. Des weiteren ist die proaktive Interferenz von zu vergessendem auf zu merkendes Material vermindert.

Während man sich heute weitgehend einig ist, daß bei der Listenmethode vor allem eine Hemmung des Abrufes der zu vergessenden Liste den Hauptmechanismus des intentionalen Vergessens darstellt, gibt es bezüglich der Wortmethode weiterhin Kontroversen. Die Mehrheit der derzeit auf diesem Gebiet tätigen Forscher geht von einer differentiellen Enkodierung der Wörter im Sinne von tiefer und flacher Verarbeitung aus (z.B. Basden et al., 1993; Basden & Basden, 1998; Wilson & Kipp, 1998). Dennoch wurden einige Ergebnisse veröffentlicht, die sich mit ausschließlich differentiellen Enkodiermechanismen nicht erklären lassen (z. B. Geiselman und Bagheri, 1985; MacLeod, 1989). Daher wurde von einigen Forschern auch für die Wortmethode zusätzlich ein Inhibitionsmechanismus angenommen, der den Zugriff auf die zu vergessenden Gedächtnisinhalte erschwert. Davon ausgehend, wurde die Wortmethode auch zur Untersuchung der Inhibitionsleistungen bei älteren Menschen (Zacks et al., 1996) und bei Probanden nach pharmakologischer Intervention (Müller & Mecklinger, 1998) herangezogen. Die vorliegende Arbeit untersucht die Mechanismen des intentionalen Vergessens in der Wortmethode.

Methoden

Mit Hilfe ereigniskorrelierter Potentiale sollte untersucht werden, welche Mechanismen dem intentionalen Vergessen bei der Wortmethode zugrunde liegen, entweder ausschließliche differentielle Enkodierung oder ein zusätzliche Hemmung des Gedächtnisabrufs. Ereigniskorrelierte Potentiale stellen elektrophysiologische Korrelate der Hirnaktivität dar und können wegen ihrer hohen zeitlichen Auflösung sehr gut für die Erforschung von

Gedächtnisprozessen genutzt werden. Leitet man EKPs bei einer Wiedererkennungsaufgabe ab, läßt sich ein sogenannter alt/neu Effekt nachweisen. Das bedeutet, daß die EKP-Kurve für wiedererkannte alte Wörter im Vergleich zu richtig zurückgewiesenen neuen Wörtern ab einer Latenz von etwa 300 ms einen positiveren Verlauf hat. Es wurden in den letzten Jahren einige zeitlich und skalptopographisch unterschiedliche Subkomponenten dieses alt/neu Effektes identifiziert, die als Korrelate von Gedächtnisphänomenen wie z.B. Familiarität, bewußter Wiedererkennung und Weiterverarbeitung der abgerufenen Gedächtnisinhalte gewertet wurde.

In zwei Experimenten mit gleichem Wortmaterial wurden jeweils 20 Probanden in einer Lernphase 180 kategoriell geordnete Nomen dargeboten. Ein zeitlich verzögert präsentierter Hinweis zeigte an, ob das jeweilige Wort zu merken oder zu vergessen (Experiment 1) beziehungsweise tief oder flach (Experiment 2) zu verarbeiten war. In einem verzögerten Wiedererkennungstest mit Präsentation 180 neuer Wörter wurden die EKPs von 61 Skalpelektroden abgeleitet. In Experiment 1 wurden zusätzlich die EKPs während der Enkodierung analysiert.

Hypothesen

Das Hauptanliegen war ein Vergleich der zeitlichen und räumlichen Muster der alt/neu Effekte im EKP in beiden Experimenten. Das bedeutet, die elektrophysiologischen Korrelate der Hirnaktivität beim intentionalen Vergessen (dessen zugrundeliegende Mechanismen entweder differentielle Enkodierung allein oder zusätzliche Inhibierung des Gedächtnisabrufs sind) wurden verglichen mit den EKP-Korrelaten der Hirnaktivität bei einer Manipulation der Verarbeitungstiefe, die eine Operationalisierung der differentiellen Enkodierung darstellt. Im Falle, daß sowohl im Experiment mit intentionalem Vergessen als auch nach Manipulation der Enkodierungtiefe gleiche zeitlich-topographische Muster der alt/neu Effekte evoziert werden, gäbe es keine Hinweise für verschiedene neuronale Mechanismen beim Abruf des studierten Materials in beiden Experimenten. Dieses Ergebnis würde das Modell der differentiellen Enkodierung unterstützen. Werden dagegen unterschiedliche Muster der alt/neu Effekte erhalten, kann das als Hinweis gewertet werden, daß sich die neuronalen Mechanismen beim Abruf der Gedächtnisinhalte in beiden Experimenten zumindest teilweise voneinander unterscheiden. Dieses Ergebnis würde also für das Modell der Inhibierung des Gedächtnisabrufes sprechen.

Ergebnisse

Die Wiedererkennensraten für zu merkende und tief enkodierte Wörter lagen bei 89 %, für zu vergessende bei 59 % und für flach enkodierte bei 73 %. Die EKPs zeigten für richtig wiedererkannte Wörter verglichen mit richtig zurückgewiesenen neuen Wörtern mindestens drei topographisch und zeitlich verschiedene positive alt/neu Effekte mit frontomedianem, parietalem und rechtsfrontalem Maximum. Während sich diese EKP-Effekte für tief und flach enkodierte Wörter entsprechend der Verarbeitungstiefe nur quantitativ unterschieden, gab es sowohl quantitative als auch qualitative Unterschiede zwischen den alt/neu Effekten beim Wiedererkennen zu merkender und zu vergessender Wörter. Insbesondere war bei zu vergessenden Wörtern der parietale alt/neu Effekt nicht nachweisbar und eine späte rechtsfrontale Positivierung stärker ausgeprägt als bei zu merkenden Wörtern.

Diskussion

Ein Vergleich der beiden Experimente ergibt, daß die Annahme unterschiedlicher Verarbeitungstiefen bei der Enkodierung zu merkender und zu vergessender Wörter nicht zur Erklärung der EKP-Phänomene beim intentionalen Vergessen genügt. Da die zeitlich-räumlichen Muster der EKPs in beiden Experimenten unterschiedlich sind, können nicht ausschließlich dieselben neuronalen Mechanismen (also differentielle Enkodierung) aktiv gewesen sein. Die Ergebnisse unterstützen daher die Annahme, daß bei der Wortmethode des intentionalen Vergessens neben der differentiellen Enkodierung auch die Hemmung des Gedächtnisabrufs eine Rolle spielt. Die Abwesenheit des parietalen und die deutliche Amplitudenerhöhung des späten rechtsfrontalen alt/neu Effektes können als Korrelate des erschwerten Zugriffs auf inhibierte Gedächtnisinhalte betrachtet werden.

Mittels ereigniskorrelierter Potentiale konnte ein Beitrag zum Verständnis der menschlichen Gedächtnisprozesse geleistet werden. Zusätzlich ergibt sich die Möglichkeit des Einsatzes der Wortmethode des intentionalen Vergessens in der klinischen Forschung. Mit diesem Paradigma können bei gleichzeitiger Ableitung der EKPs die Fähigkeit zur Unterdrückung irrelevanter Information, also zur Interferenzabwehr, bei verschiedenen neuropsychiatrischen Erkrankungen und Hirnläsionen quantifiziert und neue Erkenntnisse über die pathophysiologischen Mechanismen gewonnen werden.

References

Allan, K., Wilding, E., and Rugg, M. D. (1998): Electrophysiological evidence for dissociable processes contributing to recollection. *Acta Psychol.* 98, 231-252.

Allison, T., Wood, C. C., and McCarthy, G. M. (1986): The central nervous system. In: Coles, M. G. H., Donchin, E., and Porges, S. (Eds.), *Psychophysiology: Systems, Processes, and Applications.* New York: Guilford, 5-25.

Anderson, C. M., and Neely J. H. (1996): Interference and inhibition in memory retrieval. In: Ligon Bjork, E. and Bjork, R. A. (Eds.), *Memory.* San Diego: Academic Press, 237-313.

Atkinson, R. C. and Shiffrin, R. M. (1968): Human memory: a proposed system and its control processes. In: Spence, J. T. (Ed.), *The Psychology of Learning and Motivation: Advances in Research and Theory. Vol. 2* New York: Academic Press, 89-195.

Baddeley, A. (1995) *Working Memory.* Oxford: Clarendon Press.

Basden, B. H. and Basden, D. R. (1996): Directed forgetting: further comparisons of the item and list methods. *Memory* 4 (6), 633-653.

Basden, B. H. and Basden, D. R. (1998): Directed forgetting: a contrast of methods and interpretations. In: Golding, J. M. and MacLeod, C. M. (Eds.), *Intentional Forgetting. Interdisciplinary Approaches.* Mahwah, NJ: Lawrence Erlbaum Associates, 139-172.

Basden, B. H., Basden, D. R., and Gargano, G. J. (1993): Directed forgetting in implicit and explicit memory tests: a comparison of methods. *J Exp Psychol: Learn Mem Cogn.* 19, 603-616.

Birbaumer, N., Elbert, T., Canavan, A. G. M., and Rockstroh, B. (1990): Slow potentials of the cerebral cortex and behavior. *Psychol Rev.* 70, 1-41.

Bjork, R. A. (1970): Positive forgetting: the noninterference of items intentionally forgotten. *J Verb Learn Verb Behav.* 9, 255-268.

Bjork, R. A. (1972): Theoretical implications of directed forgetting. In: Melton, W. A. and Martin, E. (eds.) *Coding Processes in Human Memory.* Washington DC: Winston. 217-235.

Bjork, R. A. (1989): Retrieval inhibition as an adaptive mechanism in human memory. In: Roediger, H. L. and Craik, F. I. M. (Eds.): *Varieties of Memory and Consciousness: Essays in Honor of Endel Tulving.* Hillsdale, NJ: Erlbaum, 309-330.

Bjork, R. A. and Woodward, A. E. Jr. (1973): Directed forgetting of individual words in free recall. *J Exp Psychol.* 99, 22-27.

Bjork, R. A., LaBerge, D., Legrand, R. (1968): The modification of short-term memory through instructions to forget. *Psychonomic Science* 10, 55-56.

Böttcher-Gandor, C. and Ullsperger, P. (1992): Mismatch negativity in event-related potentials to auditory stimuli as a function of varying interstimulus interval. *Psychophysiology* 29(5), 546-550.

Brewer, J. B., Zhao, Z., Desmond, J. E., Glover, G. H., Gabrieli, J. D. E. (1998): Making memories: brain activity that predicts how well visual experience will be remembered. *Science* 281, 1185-1187.

Cantor, J., Engle, R. W., and Hamilton, G. (1991): Short-term memory, working memory, and verbal abilities: how do they relate? *Intelligence* 15, 229-246.

Cohen, J. (1977): *Statistical Power Analyses for the Behavioral Sciences.* New York: Academic Press.

Cohen, J. D. and Servan-Schreiber, D. (1992): Context, cortex, and dopamine: a connectionist approach to behavior and biology in schizophrenia. *Psychol Rev.* 99, 45-77.

Coles, M. G. H. (1989): Modern mind-brain reading: psychophysiology, physiology, and cognition. *Psychophysiology.* 26, 251-269.

Coles, M. G. H., Gratton, G., Kramer, A. F., and Miller, G. (1986): Principles of signal acquisition and analysis. In: Coles, M. G. H., Donchin, E., and Porges, S. (Eds.), *Psychophysiology: Systems, Processes, and Applications.* New York: Guilford, 26-44.

Cowan, N. (1988): Evolving conceptions of memory storage, selective attention, and their mutual constraints within the human information processing system. *Psychol Bull.* 104, 163-191.

Craik, F. I. M. and Lockhart, R. S. (1972): Levels of processing: a framework for memory research. *J Verb Learn Verb Behav.* 11, 671-684.

Craik, F. I. M. and Tulving, E. (1975): Depth of processing and the retention of words in episodic memory. *J Exp Psychol.* 104, 268-294.

Curran, T., Tucker, D. M., Kutas, M., and Posner, M. I. (1993): Topography of the N400: brain electrical activity reflecting expectancy. *Electroencephalogr Clin Neurophysiol.* 88, 188-209.

Donchin, E. (1981): Surprise!...Surprise? *Psychophysiology* 18, 493-513.

Donchin, E. and Coles, M. G. H. (1988): Is the P300 component a manifestation of context updating? *Behav Brain Sci.* 11, 357-372.

Donchin, E. and Fabiani, M. (1991): The use of event-related potentials in the study of memory: is P300 a measure of distinctiveness? In: Jennings, J. R. and Coles, M. G. H. (Eds.), *Handbook of Cognitive Psychophysiology: Central and Autonomic Nervous System Approaches.* London: Wiley & Sons, 471-498.

Düzel, E., Yonelinas, A. P., Mangun, G. R., Heinze H. J., and Tulving, E. (1997): Event-related brain potential correlates of two states of conscious awareness in memory. *Proc Natl Acad Sci.* 94, 5973-5978.

Epstein, W. (1972): Mechanisms of directed forgetting. In: Bower, G. H. (Ed.), *The Psychology of Learning and Motivation Vol 6*. New York: Academic Press, 147-191.

Epstein, W. and Wilder, L. (1971): Searching for to-be-forgotten material in a directed forgetting task. *J Exp Psychol.*, 95, 349-357.

Epstein, W., Massaro, D. W., and Wilder, L. (1972): Selective search in directed forgetting. *J Exp Psychol.*, 94, 18-24.

Eysenck, M. W. & Keane, M. T. (1990): *Cognitive Psychology. A Student's Handbook.* Hove, UK: Lawrence Erlbaum Associates.

Fabiani, M. and Donchin, E. (1995): Encoding processes and memory organization: a model of the von Restorff effect. *J Exp Psychol: Lean Mem Cog.* 21, 1-17.

Fabiani, M., Karis, D., and Donchin, E. (1990): Effects of mnemonic strategy manipulation in a von Restorff paradigm. *Electroencephalogr Clin Neurophysiol.* 75, 22-35.

Fechner, G. T. (1860): *Elemente der Psychophysik.* Leipzig: Druck und Verlag von Breitkopf und Härtel.

Fernández, G., Weyerts, H., Schrader-Bölsche, M., Tendolkar, I., Smid, H. G. O. M., Tempelmann, C., Hinrichs, H., Scheich, H., Elger, C. E., Mangun, G. R., and Heinze, H. J. (1998): Successful verbal encoding into episodic memory engages the posterior hippocampus: a parametrically analyzed functional magnetic resonance imaging study. *J Neurosci.* 18, 1841-1847.

Gardiner, J. M. (1988): Functional aspects of recollective experience. *Mem Cognit.* 16, 309-313.

Gardiner, J. M., Gawlik, B., Richardson-Klavehn, A. (1994): Maintenance rehearsal affects knowing, not remembering; elaborative rehearsal affects remembering, not knowing. *Psychonomic Bulletin and Review.* 1, 107-110.

Geiselman, R. E. and Bagheri, B. (1985): Repetition effects in directed forgetting: evidence for retrieval inhibition. *Mem Cognit.* 13 (1), 57-62.

Geiselman, R. E., Bjork, R. A., and Fishman, D. L. (1983): Disrupted retrieval in directed forgetting: a link with posthypnotic amnesia. *J Exp Psychol: General.* 112(1), 58-72.

Gevins, A. and Cutillo, B. (1993): Spatiotemporal dynamics of component processes in human working memory. *Electroencephalogr Clin Neurophysiol.* 87, 128-143.

Gevins, A., Cutillo, B., and Smith, M. E. (1995): Regional modulation of high resolution evoked potentials during verbal and non-verbal matching tasks. *Electroencephalogr Clin Neurophysiol.* 94, 129-147.

Gevins, A., Smith, M. E., Le, J., Leong, H., Bennett, J., Martin, M., McEvoy, L., Du, R., and Whitfield, S. (1996): High resolution evoked potential imaging of the cortical dynamics of human working memory. *Electroencephalogr Clin Neurophysiol.* 98, 327-348.

Golding, J. M. and MacLeod, C. M. (Eds.) (1998): *Intentional Forgetting. Interdisciplinary Approaches.* Mahwah, NJ: Lawrence Erlbaum Associates, 1998.

Goldman-Rakic, P. S., Bergson, C., Mrzljak, L., and Williams, G. V. (1997): Dopamine receptors and cognitive functions. In: Neve, K. A. (Ed.), *The Dopamine Receptors.* Totowa, NJ: Humana Press, 499-522.

Gratton, G. (1998): Dealing with artifacts: the EOG contamination of the event-related brain potential. *Behavior Research Methods, Instruments, and Computers* 30(1): 44-53.

Gratton, G., Coles, M. G. H., and Donchin, E. (1983): A new method for off-line removal of ocular artifact. *Electroencephalogr Clin Neurophysiol.* 55, 468-484.

Greenhouse, S. and Geisser, S. (1959): On methods in the analysis of profile data. *Psychometrika*, 24, 95-112.

Halgren, E., Baudena, P., Clarke, J. M., Heit, G., Liégeois, C., Chauvel, P., and Musolino, A. (1995): Intracerebral potentials to rare target and distractor auditory and visual stimuli. II Medial, lateral and posterior temporal pole. *Electroencephalogr Clin Neurophysiol.* 94, 229-250.

Halgren, E., Squires, N. K., Rohrbough, J. W., Babb, T. L., Crandall, P. H. (1980): Endogenous potentials generated in the human hippocampal formation and amygdala by infrequent events. *Science* 210, 803-805.

Hauselt, J. (1998): An illusion of retrieval inhibition: directed forgetting and implicit memory. In: Golding, J. M. and MacLeod, C. M. (Eds.), *Intentional Forgetting. Interdisciplinary Approaches.* Mahwah, NJ: Lawrence Erlbaum Associates, 197-218.

Hegerl, U. and Frodl-Bauch, T. (1997): Dipole source analysis of P300 component of the auditory evoked potential: a methodological advance? *Psychiatry Res.* 74(2), 109-118.

Hillyard, S. A., and Kutas, M. (1983): Electrophysiology of cognitive processing. *Annu Rev Psychol.* 34, 33-61.

Homan, R. W., Herman, J., and Purdy, P. (1987): Cerebral location of international 10-20 system electrode placement. *Electroencephalogr Clin Neurophysiol.* 66, 376-382.

Hoormann, J, Falkenstein, M, Schwarzenau, P, and Hohnsbein, J. (1998): Methods for the quantification and statistical testing of ERP differences across conditions. *Behavior Research Methods, Instruments, and Computers.* 30(1), 103-109.

Jacoby, L. L. and Kelley, C. (1992): Unconscious influences of memory: dissociations and automaticity. In: Milner, A. D. and Rugg, M. D. (Eds.), *The Neuropsychology of Consciousness.* London: Academic, 201-234.

James, W. (1890): *The Principles of Psychology. Vol. 2.* New York: Holt.

Iyo, M. and Yamasaki, T. (1993): The detection of age-related decrease of D1, D2, and serotonine 5-HT2 receptors in living human brain. *Prog Neuro-Pharmacol Biol Psychiatry.* 17, 415-421.

Johnson, H. M. (1994): Processes of successful intentional forgetting. *Psychol Bull.* 116(2), 274-292.

Johnson, R. Jr. (1993): On the neuronal generators of the P300 component of the event-related potential. *Psychophysiology.* 30, 90-97.

Johnson, R. Jr. (1995): Event-related potential insights into the neurobiology of memory systems. In: Boller, F. and Grafman, J. (Eds.), *Handbook of Neuropsychology Vol. 10*. Amsterdam, Elsevier, 135-163.

Johnson, R. Jr., Kreiter, K., Russo, B., and Zhu, J. (1998): A spatio-temporal analysis of recognition-related event-related brain potentials. *Int J Psychophysiol*. 29, 83-104.

Karis, D., Fabiani, M., and Donchin, E. (1984): "P300" and memory: individual differences in the von Restorff effect. *Cognit Psychol*. 16, 177-216.

Keppel, G., (1991): *Design and Analysis*. Englewood Cliffs, NJ, Prentice-Hall.

Knight, R. T. (1990): ERPs in patients with focal brain lesions. *Electroencephalogr Clin Neurophysiol*. 75, 72.

Knight, R. T. (1997): Distributed cortical network for visual attention. *J Cogn Neurosci*.9(1), 75-91.

Kutas, M. and Dale, A. (1997): Electrical and magnetic readings of mental functions. In: Rugg, M. D. (Ed.) *Cognitive Neuroscience*. Cambridge, MA: MIT Press, 197-242.

Kutas, M. and Federmeier, K. D. (1998): Minding the body. *Psychophysiology* 35, 135-150.

Lagerlund, T. D., Sharbrough, F. W., Jack, C. R., Erickson, B. J. , Strelow, D. C., Cicora, K. M., and Busacker, N. E. (1993): Determination of 10-20 system electrode locations using magnetic resonance image scanning with markers. *Electroencephalogr Clin Neurophysiol*. 86, 7-14.

Lang, M., Lang, W., Podreka, I., Steiner, M., Uhl, F., Suess, E., Müller, C., and Deeke, L. (1988): DC-potential shifts and regional cerebral blood flow reveal cortex involvement in human visuomotor learning. *Exp Brain Res*. 71, 353-364.

MacLeod, C. M. (1989): Directed forgetting affects both direct and indirect tests of memory. *J Exp Psychol: Learn Mem Cogn*. 15(1), 13-21.

MacLeod, C. M. (1998): Directed forgetting. In: Golding, J. M. and MacLeod, C. M. (Eds.), *Intentional Forgetting. Interdisciplinary Approaches*. Mahwah, NJ: Lawrence Erlbaum Associates, 1-58.

Massaro, D. W. and Loftus, G. R. (1996) Sensory and perceptual storage: data and theory. In: Ligon Bjork, E. and Bjork, R. A. (Eds.), *Memory*. San Diego: Academic Press, 68-99.

McCallum, W. C. and Curry, S. H. (1993): *Slow Potential Changes in the Human Brain*. New York: Plenum.

McCarthy, G. and Wood, C. C. (1985): Scalp distributions of event-related potentials: an ambiguity associated with analysis of variance models. *Electroencephalogr Clin Neurophysiol*. 62, 203-208.

McClelland, J. L., McNaughton, B. L., and O'Reilly, R. C. (1995): Why are there complementary learning systems in the hippocampuy and neocortex? Insights from the successes andfailures of connenctionist models of learning an dmemory. *Psychol Rev*. 102:419-457.

Mecklinger, A. (1998): On the modularity of recognition memory for object form and spatial location: a topographic ERP analysis. *Neuropsychologia*. 36(5), 441-460.

Mecklinger, A. and Meinshausen, R.-M. (1998): Recognition memory for object form and object location: an event-related potential study. *Mem Cognit.* 26(5), 1068-1088.

Mecklinger, A. and Müller, N. (1996): Dissociations in the processing of "what" and "where" information in working memory: an event-related potential analysis. *J Cogn Neurosci.* 8, 453-473.

Mecklinger, A. and Ullsperger, P. (1993): P3 varies with stimulus categorization rather than probability. *Electroencephalogr Clin Neurophysiol.* 86, 395-407.

Mecklinger, A. and Ullsperger, P. (1995): The P300 to novel and target events: a spatio-temporal dipole model analysis. *NeuroReport.* 7, 241-245.

Mecklinger, A., von Cramon, D. Y., and Matthes-von Cramon, G. (1998): Event-related potential evidence for specific recognition memory deficit in adult survivors of cerebral hypoxia. *Brain* 121, 1919-1935.

Mecklinger, A., Nessler, D., Penney, T., and von Cramon, D.Y. (1999): Remembering events that never happenend: dissociable brain activity for true and false recognition memory. *J Cogn Neurosci.* 11 (Suppl.), 17.

Milner, B. (1958): The memory defect in bilateral hippocampal lesions. *Psychiatry Research Reports.* 11, 109-114.

Moscovitch, M. (1992): Memory and working-with-memory: a component process model based on modules and central systems. *J Cogn Neurosci.* 4, 257-267.

Müller, U. and Mecklinger A. (1998): Inhibitory processes in directed forgetting. Behavioral and pharmacological findings. *J Cogn Neurosci.* 10 (Suppl.), 115.

Müller, U., Mecklinger A., and Ullsperger, M. (in preparation): Dopaminergic modulation of inhibitory processes in directed forgetting.

Muther, W. S. (1965): Erasure or partitioning in short-term memory. *Psychonomic Science* 3, 429-430.

Näätänen, R. (1992): *Attention and Brain Function.* Hillsdale, NJ: Lawrence Erlbaum Associates.

Näätänen, R. and Picton, T. W. (1987): The N1 wave of human electric and magnetic response to sound: a review and an analysis of the component structure. *Psychophysiology* 24, 375-425.

Neville, H., Kutas, M., Chesney, G., and Schmidt, A. L. (1986): Event-related potential during initial encoding and recognition of congruous and incongruous words. *Journal of Memory and Language.* 25, 75-92.

Nunez, P. L. (1981): *Electric Fields in the Brain: The Neurophysics of EEG.* New York: Oxford University Press.

Oken, B. S. and Chiappa, K. H. (1986): Statistical issues concerning computerized analysis of brainwave topography. *Ann Neurol.* 19, 493-494.

Okubo, Y., Suhara, T., Suzuki, K., Kobayashi, K., Inoue, O., Terasaki, O., Someya, Y., Sassa, T., Matsushima, E., Iyo, M., Tateno, Y., and Toru, M. (1997): Decreased prefrontal dopamine D1 receptors in schizophrenia revealed by PET. *Nature* 385, 634-636.

Opitz, B., Mecklinger, A., von Cramon, D. Y., and Kruggel, F. (1999): Combining electrophysiological and hemodynamic measures of the auditory oddball. *Psychophysiology* 36, 142-147.

Paller, K. A. (1990): Recall and stem-completion have different electrophysiological correlates and are modified differentially by directed forgetting. *J Exp Psychol: Learn Mem Cogn.* 16, 1021-1032.

Paller, K. A. and Kutas, M. (1992): Brain potentials during memory retrieval provide neurophysiological support for the discrimination between conscious recollection and priming. *J Cogn Neurosci.* 4(4), 375-390.

Paller, K. A., Kutas, M., and Mayes, A. R. (1987a): Neuronal correlates of encoding in an incidental learning paradigm. *Electroencephalogr Clin Neurophysiol.* 67, 360-371.

Paller, K. A., Kutas, M., Shimamura, A. P., and Squire, L. R. (1987b): Brain responses to concrete and abstract words reflect processes that correlate with later performance on a test of stem-completion priming. *Electroencephalogr Clin Neurophysiol.* Suppl. 40, 360-365.

Paller, K. A., McCarthy, G., and Wood, C. C. (1988): ERPs predictive of subsequent recall and recognition performance. *Biol Psychol.* 26, 269-276.

Paller, K. A., Kutas, M., and McIsaac, H. K. (1995): Monitoring conscious recollection via the electrical activity of the brain. *Psychol Sci.* 6(2),107-111.

Penney, T. B., Mecklinger, A., Nessler, D., and Maess, B. (1999): Possible and impossible objects evoke frontal and parietal event-related potential differences in an immediate repetition paradigm. *J Cogn Neurosci.* 11 (Suppl.), 38.

Perrin, F., Pernier, J., Bertrand, O., and Echallier, J. F. (1989): Spherical splines for scalp potential and current density mapping. *Electroencephalogr Clin Neurophysiol.* 72, 184-187.

Pfeifer, E. (1993): IPCM - Iterative PCA correction method. A new method for the correction of ocular artifacts in ERP-data. *Psychophysiology* 30, 51.

Ranganath, C. and Paller, K. (1999): Frontal brain potentials during recognition are modulated by requirements to retrieve perceptual detail. *Neuron* 22, 605-613.

Regan, D. (1989): *Human Brain Electrophysiology: Evoked Potentials and Evoked Magnetic Fields in Science and Medicine.* Amsterdam: Elsevier.

Ribot, T. A. (1882): *Diseases of Memory: An Essay in the Positive Psychology.* New York: Appleton-Century-Crofts.

Rugg, M. D. (1995): ERP studies of memory. In: Rugg, M. D. and Coles, M. G. H. (Eds.), *Electrophysiology of Mind, Event-related Brain Potentials and Cognition.* Oxford: Oxford University Press, 132-170.

Rugg, M. D. and Coles, M. G. H. (1995): The ERP and cognitive psychology: conceptual issues. In: Rugg, M. D. and Coles, M. G. H. (Eds.), *Electrophysiology of Mind, Event-related Brain Potentials and Cognition.* Oxford: Oxford University Press, 27-39.

Rugg, M. D., Fletcher, P. C., Allan, K., Frith, C.D., Frackowiak, R. S. J., and Dolan, R. J. (1998a): Neural correlates of memory retrieval during recognition memory and cued recall. *NeuroImage* 8, 262-273.

Rugg, M. D., Mark, R. E., Walla, P., Schloerscheidt, A. M., Birch, C. S., and Allan, K. (1998b): Dissociation of the neural correlates of implicit and explicit memory. *Nature* 392, 595-598.

Rugg, M. D., Schloerscheidt, A. M, and Mark, R E. (1998c): An electrophysiological comparison of two indices of recollection. *Journal of Memory and Language* 39, 47-69.

Rugg, M. D., Walla, P, Schloerscheidt, A. M., Fletcher, P. C., Frith, C. D., and Dolan, R. J. (1998d): Neural correlates of depth of processing effects on recollection: evidence from brain potentials and positron emission tomography. *Exp Brain Res.* 123, 18-23.

Sanquist, T. F., Rohrbaugh, J. W., Syndulko, K., and Lindsley, D. B. (1980): Electrophysiological signs of levels of processing: perceptual analysis and recognition memory. *Psychophysiology* 17, 568-576.

Schacter, D. L. (1987): Memory, amnesia and frontal lobe dysfunction. *Psychobiology* 15:21-36.

Schacter, D. L. (1995): Implicit memory: a new frontier for cognitive neuroscience. In: Gazzaniga, M. S. (Ed.), *The Cognitive Neurosciences.* Cambridge, MA: MIT Press, 815-824.

Schacter, D. L. (1997): The cognitive neuroscience of memory: perspectives from neuroimaging research. *Phil Trans R Soc Lond.* 352, 1689-1695.

Schacter, D. L., and Graf, P. (1986): Effects of elaborative processing on implicit and explicit memory for new associations. *J Exp Psychol: Learn Mem Cogn.* 12, 432-444.

Scherg, M. and von Cramon, D. Y. (1986): Evoked dipole source potentials of the human auditory cortex. *Electroencephalgr Clin Neurophysiol.* 65, 344-360.

Senkfor, A. J. and Van Petten, C. (1998): Who said what? An event-related potential investigation of source and item memory. *J Exp Psychol: Learn Mem Cogn.* 24, 1005-1025.

Sharbrough, F., Chatrian, G., Lesser, R. P., Lüders, H., Nuwer, M., and Picton, T.W. (1990): *Guidelines for Standard Electrode Position Nomenclature.* Bloomfield, American EEG Society.

Shebilske, W., Wilder, L., and Epstein, W. (1971): Effect of forget instructions with and without the conditions for selective search. *Mem Cognit.* 1, 261-267.

Shimamura, A. P (1995): Memory and frontal lobe function. In: Gazzaniga, M. S. (Ed.), *The Cognitive Neurosciences.* Cambridge, MA: MIT Press, 803-813.

Shimamura, A. P, and Squire, L. R. (1987): A neuropsychological study of fact memory and source amnesia. *J Exp Psychol: Learn Mem Cogn.* 13, 464-473.

Shimamura, A. P., Jurica, P. J., Mangels, J. A., Gershberg, F. B., and Knight, R. T. (1995): Susceptibility to memory interference effects following frontal lobe damage - findings from tests of paired-associate learning. *J Cogn Neurosci.* 7, 144-1525.

Smith, M. E. (1993): Neurophysiological manifestation of recollective experience during recognition memory judgments. *J Cogn Neurosci.* 5, 1-13.

Somjen, G. G. (1973): Electrogenesis of sustained potentials. *Prog Neurobiol.* 1, 199-237.

Spencer, K. M., Vila, E., and Donchin, E. (1994): ERPs and performance measures reveal individual differences in a recollection/familiarity task. *Psychophysiology* 31, 93.

Spitzer, M. (1997): A cognitive neuroscience view of schizophrenic thought disorder. *Schizophr Bull.* 21, 29-50.

Squire, L. R. and Knowlton, B. J. (1995): Memory, hippocampus, and brain systems. In: Gazzaniga, M. S. (Ed.), *The Cognitive Neurosciences.* Cambridge, MA: MIT Press, 825-837.

Squire, L. R. and Zola, S. M. (1996): Structure and function of declarative and nondeclarative memory systems. *Proc Natl Acad Sci.* 93, 13515-13522.

Stuss, D. T., Eskes, G. A., Foster, J. K. (1994):. Experimental neuropsychological studies of frontal lobe functions. In: Boller, F. and Grafman, J. (Eds.) *Handbook of Neuropsychology, Vol 9.* Amsterdam: Elsevier, 149-183.

Timmins, W. K. (1974): Varying processing time in directed forgetting. *Journal of Verbal Learning and Verbal Behavior* 13, 539-544.

Towle, V. L., Bolaños, J., Suarez, D., Tan, K., Grzeszczuk, R., Levin, D. N., Cakmur, R., Frank, S. A., & Spire, J-P. (1993): The spatial location of EEG electrodes: locating best-fitting sphere relative to cortical anatomy. *Electroencephalogr Clin Neurophysiol.* 86, 1-6.

Tulving, E. (1985): Memory and consciousness. *Canadian Psychologist.* 26, 1-12.

Tulving, E. (1995): Organization of memory: quo vadis? In: Gazzaniga, M. S. (Ed.), *The Cognitive Neurosciences.* Cambridge, MA: MIT Press, 839-847.

Ullsperger, P. and Mecklinger, A. (1996): P300 as an index of cognitive adaptation. In Ogura, C., Koga, Y., and Shimikochi, M. (Eds.) *Recent Advances in Event-related Potentials: Proceedings of the 11th International Conference on Event-related Potentials (EPIC).* Amsterdam: Elsevier, 47-51.

von Restorff, H. (1933): Über die Wirkung von Bereichsbildungen im Spurenfeld. *Psychologische Forschung* 18, 299-342.

Wagner, A. D., Desmond, J. E., Glover, G. H., and Gabrieli, J. D. E. (1998a): Prefrontal cortex and recognition memory. Functional-MRI evidence for context-dependent retrieval processes. *Brain* 121, 1985-2002.

Wagner, A. D, Schacter, D., Rotte, M., Koutstaal, W., Maril, A., Dale, A. M., Rosen, B. R., and Buckner, R. L. (1998b): Building memories: remembering and forgetting of verbal experiences as predicted by brain activity. *Science* 281, 1188-1191.

Weiner, B. (1968): Motivated forgetting and the study of repression. *J Pers.* 36, 213-234.

Weiner, B., and Reed, H. (1969): Effects of the instructional sets to remember and to forget on short-term retention: studies of rehearsal control and retrieval inhibition (repression). *J Exp Psychol.* 79:226-232.

Wetzel, C. D. (1975): Effects of orienting tasks and cue timing on the free recall of remember- and forget-cued words. *J Exp Psychol: Hum Learn*, 1:556-566.

Wetzel, C. D., Hunt, R. E. (1977): Cue delay and role of rehearsal in directed forgetting. *J Exp Psychol: Hum Learn.* 3, 233-245.

Wilding, E. L. and Rugg, M. D. (1996): An event-related potential study of recognition memory with and without retrieval of source. *Brain* 119, 889-905.

Wilding, E. L. and Rugg, M. D. (1997): Event-related potentials and the recognition memory exclusion task. *Neuropsychologia* 35, 119-128.

Wilding, E. L., Doyle, M. C., and Rugg, M. D. (1995): Recognition memory with and without retrieval of context: an event-related potential study. *Neuropsychologia* 33, 743-767.

Wilson, S. P. and Kipp, K. (1998): The development of efficient inhibition: evidence from directed-forgetting tasks. *Dev Rev.* 18, 86-123.

Wood, C. C. (1987): Generators of event-related potentials. In A. M. Halliday, S. R. Butler, and R. Paul (Eds.), *A Textbook of Clinical Neurophysiology.* New York: Wiley, 535-567.

Woodward, A. E. Jr., and Bjork, R. A. (1971): Forgetting and remembering in free recall: intentional and unintentional. *J Exp Psychol.* 89, 109-116.

Woodward, A. E. Jr., Bjork, R. A., and Jongeward, R. H. Jr. (1973): Recall and recognition as a function of primary rehearsal. *Journal of Verbal Learning and Verbal Behavior* 12, 608-617.

Yonelinas, A. P. and Jacoby, L. L. (1994): Dissociations of processes in recognition memory: effects of interference and of response speed. *Can J Exp Psychol.* 48, 516-534.

Zacks, R. T. and Hasher, L. (1994):. Directed Ignoring. Inhibitory Regulation of working memory. In: Dagenbach, D. and Carr, T. H. (Eds.), *Inhibitory Processes in Attention, Memory, and Language.* San Diego: Academic Press, 241-264.

Zacks, R. T., Radvansky, G., and Hasher, L. (1996): Studies of directed forgetting in older adults. *J Exp Psychol: Learn Mem Cogn.* 22, 143-156.

Erklärung über die eigenständige Abfassung der Arbeit

Hiermit erkläre ich, daß ich die vorliegende Arbeit selbständig und ohne unzulässige Hilfe oder Benutzung anderer als der angegebenen Hilfsmittel angefertigt habe. Ich versichere, daß Dritte von mir weder unmittelbar noch mittelbar geldwerte Leistungen für Arbeiten erhalten haben, die im Zusammenhang mit der vorgelegten Dissertation stehen, und daß die vorgelegte Arbeit weder im Inland noch im Ausland in gleicher oder ähnlicher Form einer anderen Prüfungsbehörde zum Zweck einer Promotion oder eines anderen Prüfungsverfahrens vorgelegt wurde. Alles aus anderen Quellen und von anderen Personen übernommene Material, das in der Arbeit verwendet wurde oder auf das direkt Bezug genommen wird, wurde als solches kenntlich gemacht. Insbesondere wurden alle Personen erwähnt, die direkt an der Entstehung der vorliegenden Arbeit beteiligt waren.

Leipzig, 1. August 1999

Markus Ullsperger

Curriculum Vitae

Name:	Markus Ullsperger
Date of birth:	April 22, 1970
born in:	Berlin, Germany

1976 - 1986	Polytechnical School in Berlin
1986 - 1988	Extended Secondary School (High school) in Halle (Saale), preparation for studies in the Czech Republic
1988 - 1989	Military service
Sept. 1989 - Aug. 1993	Studies of medicine at the Medical faculty of the Charles-University in Pilsen, Czech Republic
Sept. 1993 - Sept. 1996	Studies of medicine at the Charité - Medical faculty of the Humboldt-University in Berlin
Sept. - Oct. 1994	Elective in surgery and orthopedics at the Mercy Medical Center, Springfield, Ohio, USA
Sept. 1995 - Sept. 1996	Senior electives in Berlin and for two months in general surgery and neurosurgery at the Ohio State University Medical Center, Columbus, Ohio, USA
1996	Final examinations in medicine, mark of distinction
Oct. 1996 - April 1998	Internship at the Department of Neurology, Klinik Bosse, Lutherstadt Wittenberg, Germany
April 1998	Approbation as physician
May 1998 - Aug. 1999	Dissertation at the Max Planck Institute of Cognitive Neuroscience, Leipzig, Germany; supported by a scholarship (grant S118) of the Gertrud Reemtsma Stiftung bei der Max-Planck-Gesellschaft
since Aug. 1999	Scientific staff member of the Max Planck Institute of Cognitive Neuroscience, Leipzig, Germany; department of neurology, group 'functional neuroanatomy of the frontal lobes'

MPI Series in Cognitive Neuroscience